WORLD
OF
BUSINESS

AN INTERMEDIATE COURSE
IN BUSINESS ENGLISH

DAVID COTTON

Senior Lecturer in English as a Foreign Language,
City of London Polytechnic

Language Practice by Jocelyn Neuman

Nelson

Thomas Nelson and Sons Limited
Nelson House   Mayfield Road
Walton-on-Thames
Surrey   KT12 5PL   UK

51 York Place
Edinburgh
EH1 3JD   UK

Thomas Nelson (Hong Kong) Limited
Toppan Building 10/F
22A Westlands Road
Quarry Bay   Hong Kong

First published by Unwin Hyman Limited 1984
(Under ISBN 0 7135 1413 2)
Reprinted three times

Second impression published by Thomas Nelson and Sons Limited 1989

ISBN 0-17-555855-8
NPN 9 8 7 6 5

Text and illustrations prepared by Orlando Language Texts Ltd.
Phototypeset by Quadraset Limited, Radstock, Avon.
Printed and bound in Great Britain by M & A Thomson Litho Ltd, East Kilbride.

To my daughter Gisèle for choosing the title

Acknowledgements

The publishers are grateful to the following for permission to reproduce photographs
on the pages indicated:

page 1, Honeywell; page 11, Gloria Vanderbilt for Murjani; page 18, The Stock
Exchange; page 27, De Bijenkorf, Amsterdam; page 36, Brazilian Embassy, London;
page 44, Mabushita Electric Company; page 51, Peter Newark's Western Americana;
pages 59, 61 and 66, Skis Rossignol; page 69, McDonald's Hamburgers Ltd; page 77,
Malayan Rubber Fund Board; page 97, Gil and Ann Loescher; page 119, Royal
Arsenal Co-operative Society Ltd; page 127, De Beers Consolidated Mines Ltd.

Drawings by Von Whiteman and Stephen Essex.

CONTENTS

INTRODUCTION

This course is designed for those who already have a basic knowledge of English and now wish to acquire the specialized vocabulary and language skills of business.

It consists of 15 units, each one based on an aspect of business. The text may be about a new trend, a dramatic event, a controversial issue or the problems facing a particular company. The topics cover a wide range of subjects and are international in scope.

A typical unit includes discussion work; reading and listening comprehension; vocabulary-building exercises; review and practice of points of grammar; presentation of language functions; a problem involving a role play or simulation exercise; additional discussion topics and a writing assignment.

The teacher's book contains tapescripts for the listening comprehension exercises and keys to the exercises. A cassette with recordings of the dialogues and listening comprehension passages is also available.

AIMS OF THE COURSE
—to teach and practise the language of business;
—to develop communication skills necessary for business careers;
—to revise basic grammatical structures and patterns of English in a business context;
—to practise the four language skills—reading, speaking, listening and writing;
—to extend students' knowledge of the world of business by presenting texts about new trends, significant developments and the problems and successes of individual organizations;
—to ensure that the contexts within which the language is practised are drawn from a number of different countries or areas of the world.

EACH UNIT HAS THE FOLLOWING SECTIONS:

To Start You Talking
One or two questions related to the subject matter of the text are suggested for discussion. Students are prepared for the reading passage and cover some of the vocabulary in it.

The Text
Most passages are about 450–500 words in length. Those towards the end of the book are slightly longer and more difficult to read. The average student at this level should be able to read a text in 10–15 minutes. The reading passage provides a context for the grammatical structures dealt with in the unit, and all sections are linked either directly or indirectly to the central topic.

Comprehension

The questions in this section are intended for group discussion and test whether students have understood the main ideas of the passage. One question generally requires the student to explain the meaning of certain words or phrases in the text. Some questions are more subtle; for example, the reader is asked to interpret meaning, or to give an opinion about a statement.

Vocabulary

There are two vocabulary exercises in each unit. The first is usually based on terms that have already appeared in the text; the second introduces new items. This section aims at enriching students' vocabulary. Some of the exercises are gap-filling ones; others involve completing a passage with suitable words, or providing correct noun and adjective forms for given words. A few are open-ended; for example, in one exercise students must comment on a graph, using expressions which describe changes in the price of a share.

Language Practice

This section consists of exercises focusing on points of grammar which cause particular difficulty. They are constructed in such a way that they encourage students to respond actively, usually orally. Many exercises require learners to interpret visual material, for example charts, statistics or graphs.

Oral Work

1. *Dialogue*

The dialogues are fairly short and may be listened to or read out by the students. The purpose of the dialogue is to prepare the learner for the *problem*. It does this in two ways. First, it introduces the language functions which the student needs to participate effectively in the problem-solving activity. Second, it sets up a problem, providing information which can be used to solve it. Following each dialogue, the language functions are listed. Then students do a short exercise to practise using them.

2. *Problem*

In this section, students are presented with a problem to solve under the heading 'What do you think?' Usually, they are instructed to hold a meeting, the purpose of which is to discuss the problem and work out appropriate courses of action. In many units, the discussions involve role play or simulation activities.

The problems often contain an element of confrontation, involving groups of people, or individuals, who have different ideas about how to deal with a situation—this commonly gives rise to lively discussions. This is an important section because it gives students the opportunity to practise the vocabulary, structures and language functions which they have learned in earlier sections.

Additional Discussion Topics

Students discuss themes related to the text or issues developed in the problem-solving section.

Writing Exercise

Most of these exercises are based on common business procedures. Students are required to write memoranda, business letters and telexes, and to draft advertisements and notices.

Listening Comprehension

Most of the recordings consist of dialogues, but other kinds of listening material are included, such as excerpts from lectures, sales presentations, radio and television programmes, and telephone conversations. The exercises are task-based: while listening to the tape, for example, students must note down facts and figures which are later used to complete a chart, a memorandum or a newspaper article. A few exercises are of the traditional kind where students answer questions based on the listening passage.

1 CHANGES IN THE OFFICE

'The type of work and the activities of office workers have not changed much in the past 20 years.' Do you agree with this statement? Give reasons for your answer.

Modern office equipment: Honeywell information systems in use.

1

As most managers know, it is not always easy to persuade staff to use new machines, or to accept changes in their working conditions. The management may truly believe that the machines or changes are for the good of their employees. The employees, however, often think differently.

5 Here is an example to illustrate the point. This story is about a large insurance company in Europe. Its head office is situated in a major city. About five years ago, the company had a problem. The amount of paperwork in the office was increasing and the clerical workers were having trouble dealing with it. Unfortunately, the company could not employ more workers because office space was
10 limited.

To solve the problem, the management decided to change the location of their head office by moving to a town about 50 kilometres away. They also had another reason for wanting to move: the company was losing 16% of working hours because staff were arriving late to work. They were often delayed by the unreliable
15 transport system in the city.

While the management were planning the move, they held frequent talks with trade union representatives and junior managers in the company. In addition, they promised that the employees would keep their jobs after the move.

In fact, the planned move did not take place. Instead, the management decided
20 to improve productivity by various means. First, over a period of two years, they introduced word processors into the office. These are, essentially, highly developed electronic typewriters. They save the time of secretaries and typists, and make them more productive.

The company made two other changes. It divided the clerical workers into word-
25 processor operators and ordinary clerks. And, to reduce the number of lost working hours, it introduced 'flexitime'. Staff were allowed to vary the times they arrived at their office, and left it. However, the time they actually spent at their desks was automatically recorded.

The effect of the changes on the office supervisors and clerks was surprising.
30 The supervisors who were not in charge of word-processor operators felt that their jobs were less important. They also believed that automatic recording of attendance reduced their authority. Before, it was *they* who controlled employees' attendance.

The employees were not happy either. They thought that the management had
35 introduced word processors to 'squeeze' more work out of them. They particularly disliked the flexitime system. The company had tried to sell it to them as an employee benefit, but the staff preferred the old way of controlling attendance. Supervisors had always been 'reasonable' if someone wanted to arrive at work late, or leave early.

A Comprehension

1. What problems did the insurance company have? How did it try to solve them? ① the amount of paperwork was increasing ② The company was losing 16% of w/h

2. What did the management do to prepare staff for the move? They held frequent talks with ...

3. Why didn't the mangement change the location of their head office? because, they'd decided to improve productivity by others ways.

4. How does a word processor help a secretary to be more efficient? It helps a secretary because it contains the information in its Disc.

2

5. Why did the supervisors and clerical workers dislike flexitime?

SUPERVISOR → JOBS LESS IMPORTANT , CLERICAL WORKERS weren't reasonable

6. Explain clearly the meaning of these words and phrases:

paperwork (l. 7)
junior managers (l. 17)
improve productivity (l. 20)
authority (l. 32)
sell it as an employee benefit (l. 36)

B Vocabulary

1. In this passage, a secretary describes her work. Use some of her words and phrases to match the meanings given below.

   'I work as secretary to the director of an export company. My boss is Mr Wood. We're doing a lot of business at the moment, so I'm always up to my eyes in work. You see, my job isn't just sorting out the mail, typing letters and filing documents. I have many other duties. For example, our office receives a lot of routine correspondence, which I usually deal with. I also draft important letters and memoranda for Mr Wood, as well as organize his diary and work schedule. We've got a large number of overseas customers, so I'm continually sending telexes and cables abroad. In addition to that, I have to take telephone calls, handle travel and hotel bookings, and entertain visitors. Oh yes, I forgot to mention, I'm responsible for buying office supplies too.
   My boss is interested in business machines. He's got a dictating machine and intercom on his desk. In the corner of the office, there's his new toy—a micro-computer. Now he's keen to buy a word processor. I suppose I'll have to learn how to use that soon.'

Meaning	*Word/phrase*
a firm which sells its goods overseas	EXPORT COMPANY
a person in control of others	BOSS
very busy	UP TO MY EYES
storing papers	FILING DOCUMENTS
letters which an office normally receives and must reply to	ROUTINE CORRESPONDENCE
notes sent from one person or office to another within the same company	MEMORANDA
write in rough form	DRAFT
deal with	TO HANDLE
amuse and interest	T.O. ENTERTAIN

a means of speaking to several offices linked to each other by means of microphones and loudspeakers

Intercom

a machine for storing and printing text that has been typed into it

Word Processor

2. Here are some things you can find in an office:

cupboard	file	in-tray	3 stapler
4 chart	1 filing cabinet	6 out-tray	10 telex
desk	folder	7 keyboard	wastepaper
5 diary	flimsy	3 paper clip	9 basket/bin
2 drawing pin	floppy disc	8 safe	shredder

Which do you use to . . . ?

1 store records
2 stick notices on a board
3 hold papers together (two possible answers)
4 show figures or graphs
5 note down appointments
6 hold letters and memos that will soon be sent
7 type in information
8 keep money and valuable documents
9 throw things into which you no longer need
10 pass printed messages from one place to another

What do you use the other things for?

C Language Practice

Word processors *save* the time of secretaries and typists, and *make* them more productive.
The present simple tense is used here to express facts which are permanently true.

Read the following:
Mr Corbett, the manager of a small company, answered this advertisement.

WORD WONDER
YOUR OFFICE OF THE FUTURE FOR ONLY £500
You know that the cost of producing typed paperwork is becoming an expensive item in your office expenditure.
What you need is the Word Wonder word processor.
Ring 11-222 3333 to arrange a visit by one of our representatives.

Before the Word Wonder representative's visit, Mr Corbett made a list of things he wanted to find out.

List of questions to ask Word Wonder representative

Find out:

1. DOGS   If the machine shows ~~one~~ *you* completed page of a long document?
2. How many standard letters and documents the machine memorizes? DOGS
3. DOGS   If the machine puts words or paragraphs in new positions?
4. If we can put a whole block of text on another page.
5. How much the machine gets on one page. DOGS
6. DOGS   If the machine wipes off words or characters.[1]
7. DOGS   How fast the machine prints.
8. DOGS   If the machine matches names and addresses to standard letters.

This is the list of information the Word Wonder representative looked at in order to answer Mr Corbett's questions.

Word Wonder Specifications

5   118 characters per line, 100 lines per page.
1   Screen display of any completed page of document or letter.
2   Storage of up to 200 pre-set documents or letters.
3   Repositioning of whole paragraphs or single words.
6   Removal of single characters, words or paragraphs.
4   Movement of blocks of text from one page to another.
8   Automatic filing of names and addresses with standard letters.
7   Printing rate: 160 characters per second.

Mr Corbett's meeting with the representative started like this:

Mr Corbett: There are several things I'd like to know about your word processor.

Representative: Yes, Mr Corbett.

Mr Corbett: Does the machine show one completed page of a long document?

Representative: A screen displays any completed page.

Work in pairs

Ask and answer Mr Corbett's other questions.

---

[1]Characters = single letters, i.e. a, b, c.

5

D Oral Work

Preparation   Making suggestions

Susan and Jane work as clerk-typists in an insurance company. The manager of the office is Mr Harris. Read or listen to the dialogue.

Susan: Jane, do you know what I've just heard?

Jane: Not bad news, I hope.

Susan: It is, actually. I was talking to Pat a few minutes ago. You know she's friendly with Mr Harris . . .

Jane: Yes, I believe they do get on rather well.

Susan: Well, Mr Harris told Pat in confidence. Um . . .

Jane: Yes, go on.

Susan: All right. Pat told me the management's going to make big changes in our office. They're going to put everything on a computer—filing, accounts, wages, the lot.

Jane: Good heavens! You mean, they're planning to computerize the whole department?

Susan: Exactly. And when that happens, we'll be out of a job.

Jane: Mmm . . . you may be right, Susan. Look, let's go and see Pat, and find out more about this.

Susan: I don't think she knows anything more.

Jane: Why don't we see Mr Harris then?

Susan: We can't do that. After all, I did promise Pat that I wouldn't tell anyone.

Jane: Yes, that's true. You know, Susan, it might be a good idea if we started looking for another job. How about calling in at the employment agency on our way home?

Practise these expressions

To make suggestions:

Examples:

Let's talk to the manager about this problem.
Why don't we introduce flexitime in our company?
It might be a good idea if we used computers to handle our accounts.

To accept/reject suggestions:

Examples:

Yes, that's a good idea.
No, that's not a good idea. (The speaker is definite.)
No, I don't think we should do that. (The speaker is less definite.)

Work in pairs. One of you is an office worker, the other is the manager of the office. Using the expressions listed below, the office worker makes suggestions for improving his/her working conditions.

Example:

A: Why don't we have a two-hour lunch break?
B: No, I don't think that's a good idea.

Let's ......
Shouldn't you ...... ?
Why not ...... ?
It might be a good idea if we ......
It might be worth/worth while ......
Why don't you/we ...... ?

Problem

Gerald Parker, managing director of Reliant Insurance plc, is unhappy. This morning, three managers have come into his office, each telling him the same story. Somehow or other, the office employees have heard about the computer systems which will soon be introduced. The employees are all very upset. The older ones are afraid of modern technology, and the younger ones do not want to learn new methods of work. Most of the staff are certain that they will lose their jobs when the office is computerized. Some are already looking for jobs with other firms.

The staff are right in one way. The company will need fewer office workers when the computer is installed. This will be in three months' time, but the machine and systems will be working efficiently only six to nine months later. At that time, about half the staff—there are 15 altogether—will have to leave because there will be no work for them.

But what about now? This is the busiest time of the year for the company. Every employee is working overtime and will continue to do so for the next two months or more. The office has recently taken on two temporary workers, but neither is doing her job well.

Mr Parker is worried. He did not tell the office staff about the plans to install a computer because, for a long time, the management were not sure if they wanted to introduce it. He still has not signed the contract with the supplier of the equipment. Now he is beginning to think 'Maybe we should forget about the computer and leave the office as it was'.

What do you think?

Mr Parker talks about the problem with some of his managers. He asks them to make suggestions and advise him what to do now.

Instructions:

Work in *small groups*. One of you is managing director, the others are managers of the company. The managing director should discuss with the other members of the meeting the following questions:

1. What actions should the management take to solve the problem?
2. Should Mr Parker try to find out *who* told the workers about his plans? If so, what action should he take?
3. Have the management made any mistakes? If so, what are they?

Additional Discussion Topics

1. 'The secretary will soon disappear from office life.' True or false?
2. This chart is based on a recent study of the work of secretaries. It shows how the average secretary spends his/her working day. Some activities are missing from it. Using the list below as a guide, put each activity in an appropriate position on the chart. (Answers in the Teacher's Book.)

Talking face to face
6% of the day
. . . . . .
8%
. . . . . .
13%
. . . . . .
20%
Coffee and personal
2%
. . . . . .
2%
. . . . . .
18%
. . . . . .
4%
. . . . . .
2%
Miscellaneous
5%
Typing
20%

List of activities
★ clerical work
★ filing
★ dictation
★ photocopying, taking messages to people
★ dealing with the post
★ talking on the telephone
★ waiting for work

E Writing Exercise

Susan Barnes is a clerk-typist at Reliant Insurance. She is an excellent worker. This morning she went to see Mr Harris, the office manager, and handed him a letter saying that she was giving up her job. Mr Harris did not want Susan to leave, so he tried to persuade her to change her mind.

Write the dialogue that took place between Susan and Mr Harris. If you wish, use the start of their conversation which is given below.

Mr Harris: I must say, Susan, I'm surprised by this letter of resignation. Why do you want to leave, exactly?

Susan: It's quite simple really, Mr Harris. You're going to computerize all the office systems soon, so there won't be any work for the clerk-typists, will there?

Mr Harris: . . . . . .

Susan: . . . . . .

F Listening Comprehension

First, listen to the dialogue. Then listen again and complete these notes.

1. Mrs Keller arranged to meet Mr Perkins because . . . .
2. Her firm is fairly large. It supplies . . . .
3. It is also a complex business. They have more than . . . .
4. One of their main problems is . . . .
5. If a book sells well, they . . . .
6. In order to get new supplies of a book, someone . . . .
7. If the company installs a computer, they will know . . . .
8. Using a computer, you can find out the number of each book in stock. You just . . . .
9. A computer will also warn you that . . . .
10. Mrs Keller would have to pay . . . . She thinks that the cost is . . . .

9

2 GLORIA VANDERBILT JEANS

Why are jeans so popular in many countries? Do you think there will always be a market for them?

Murjani is a manufacturer of high-fashion or 'designer' jeans. These are sold under the Gloria Vanderbilt label. The company's biggest market is the United States. There, Gloria Vanderbilt jeans are a household name. However, as recently as 1977, Murjani was having little success selling jeans or any other merchandise
5 in the US. Its turnover was only $25 million.

At that time, the American head of the company, Mr Warren Hirsch, had a clever idea. He decided to change the image of the jeans, priced at $10 a pair. He set out to make them status symbols, so that people wearing them would appear fashionable, well-to-do and with good taste. For these qualities, they would pay
10 $40 a pair.

To change the jeans' image, Mr Hirsch was able to persuade Gloria Vanderbilt —a member of a rich and famous American family—to endorse the product. She let the company put her name on the back pocket of the jeans. After that, he arranged for her to appear on television.
15 In television commercials, Miss Vanderbilt seemed to be promoting the jeans. Actually, she was selling an image of wealth and elegance. Obviously, young people in New York did not have her money or style but, by buying her jeans, they could look or feel as if they did.

This new approach to marketing the product was successful. After one year of
20 television advertising, Murjani's sales increased to $150 million. In the following year, they almost doubled. Naturally, the managers in Hong Kong were delighted with the results. They forecast that sales would reach $1,000 million by 1985.

Some fashion experts believe that this figure is too high. The market for expensive jeans has become very competitive now. There are over 200 firms in the
25 business, though many of these are late-comers looking for quick profits.

There is another reason why Murjani's rate of growth may slow down. Rival companies have started using television to promote their own jeans. A few years ago, jeans rarely appeared in television commercials; these days, they are frequently advertised on television in the New York area.
30 One day, the boom in jeans sales will come to an end. Manufacturers like Murjani are already preparing for that time by diversifying into other fields, such as sports goods and footwear.

Jenny Hudson models the new black magic of Gloria Vanderbilt.

A Comprehension

1. Why did Murjani change its method of marketing jeans? What kind of changes did it make?

2. What does the phrase 'to endorse the product' (1. 12) mean? Can you give other examples of people endorsing products? ᴛᴏ ɢɪᴠᴇ ᴍᴇʀ ꜱɪɢɴᴀᴛᴜʀᴇ, ᴊᴀɴɢ ꜰᴏɴᴅᴀ
   ᴄᴀʟᴠɪɴ ᴄʟᴏɪɴ

3. Why did the television commercials increase Murjani's sales of jeans?
   Because most people watch that.

4. What was Murjani's turnover for jeans after they had been advertised on television for two years?

5. In what way is the market for high-fashion jeans changing?

6. What has Murjani done to avoid depending too much on jeans sales?

11

B Vocabulary

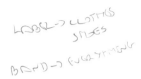

1. Complete these sentences using the words in italics. (Make any necessary changes in the form of the words.)

brand   image   label   merchandise   status   market   marketing
endorse   predict   promote

a) In 1977, Murjani changed its .... policy.

b) Television commercials, advertisements and endorsements are all means of .... goods.

c) Manufacturers use advertising to create an ...... for their products.

d) The ...... for designer jeans in the United States is worth $750 million.

e) Department stores often sell clothes under their own ....

f) Sales of a product generally increase if a famous person ...... it.

g) Not all the ...... that Murjani sells is expensive.

h) There are many different ...... of jeans on the market.

i) In many societies, clothes are a sign of a person's ....

j) It is difficult to ...... changes in fashion.

2. Working in pairs, discuss what each of the italic words or phrases mean. Then choose four of the terms and use them in your own sentences.

Most companies have advertising *budgets*. They use the money to increase sales of their products, *launch* new products, and change people's *attitudes* to their organizations.

When a company decides to carry out an *advertising campaign*, it generally contacts an expert in the field—the advertising agency. The agency plans the campaign for its *client*. For example, it carries out *market studies* and provides essential marketing *data* on which to build a campaign. It also selects the *media*—newspapers, magazines, television, posters, etc.—which will be used for promoting the product. It will advise the client how to create the right *brand image* and will invent messages or *slogans* to attract the public's attention.

The bigger agencies offer a wide range of services, so companies should get a good *return* on their investment. However, it is often difficult to *assess* accurately the effectiveness of a campaign. Most companies stay with their agency for a long time, but some advertisers change agencies regularly. They believe that, after a while, the agency loses its creative touch.

C Language Practice

Could; was/were able to

Obviously, young people in New York did not have Gloria Vanderbilt's money or style. But by buying her jeans, they *could feel* as if they did.

This means: *It was possible* for them to look or feel as if they had her money or style.

Mr Hirsh *was able to persuade* Gloria Vanderbilt to endorse the product.
    This means: *He managed to persuade* her to endorse the product.

Read the following, and complete the exercises:
Magnus, a manufacturer of jeans, launched an advertising campaign in the press. Their sales manager bargained with the publications to get the cheapest prices for placing his advertisements.
    Here is the record he kept of advertisements placed in March. He has noted the maximum number of readers for each publication and the price he paid for his advertisements.

Teenage magazines	Readership	Cost of advertisement
Your Life	320,000	Half-page £1,500
Fan Mail	480,000	Quarter-page £800
Drift	270,000	Half-page £1,200
Women's magazines		
Hers	440,000	Full-page £3,200
View	380,000	Quarter-page £900
Today	350,000	Full-page £2,000
Newspapers		
The Bell	170,000	Half-page £900
Ashley News	200,000	Quarter-page £500
The Globe	250,000	Half-page £1,000

Exercise 1

'In March the sales manager was able to buy a half-page in the teenage magazine *Your Life*.'
    Make similar comments about the other advertisements he placed in March.

Exercise 2 (Work in pairs)

Student A asks student B, the sales manager for Magnus Jeans, why he chose particular publications and how cheaply he was able to buy advertising space.

Model dialogue:

A: Why did you choose *Your Life*?

B: Because we could reach up to 320,000 readers.

A: What did you pay for the advertisement?

B: I was able to get half a page for £1,500.

Ask and answer questions about the other publications.

D Oral Work

Preparation   Giving advice/pointing out problems

Gemma Kline is the owner of Gemma Fashions, a clothing firm supplying the New York market. She is talking to Carl, her chief designer. Read or listen to the dialogue.

Gemma: I can't understand it, Carl. Why won't our turnover go over $2 million? What are we doing wrong?

Carl: I don't know. There's certainly nothing wrong with our merchandise. The customers love our designs, and they never complain about the quality or prices.

Gemma: Yes, but the stores and dress shops don't place big orders with us. That's why our turnover's sticking at two million.

Carl: I think our real problem is that we're not well known enough. People don't look at our clothes and say 'Ah, there's a Gemma Kline outfit'.

Gemma: Mmm . . . that's true.

Carl: Don't forget, there are hundreds of firms like us. They all think their goods are terrific, and they're trying to persuade people to buy them.

Gemma: All right, the competition's tough—we know that. But our clothes *are* terrific, Carl. You should know, you design them. Look at the new trouser suit. It should be a real winner.

Carl: Ah, you're not absolutely sure about the suit, are you?

Gemma: Well, you can't be a hundred per cent certain, can you?

Carl: Perhaps not . . . . You know, if I were you, Gemma, I'd spend more money on advertising this year. If this firm's going to get bigger, we've got to promote our goods better.

Gemma: You realize it'll cost a lot of money if we use an agency.

Carl: It might not be too expensive. You could try one of the smaller agencies. They'd probably be glad of the business.

Gemma: Some of the small ones are very good, it's true.

Carl: I'd advise you to talk to one or two of them. Ask them how they'd plan a campaign for us. It might be quite interesting.

Gemma: Do you know, Carl, I'll do that. You can come along with me if you like. After all, it was your idea.

Practise these expressions

To give advice:

If I were you, I'd . . .   *You could . . .*
I think you should . . .   *I'd advise you to . . .*
It might be advisable to . . .   *You really ought to . . .*

LS

ptcc of prop
unts out your
plan for ad advrtisn
camprign + quote

GLORIA VANDERBILT JEANS

Examples:

If I were you, I'd change the image of the jeans.
You could increase your advertising budget.
I'd advise you to diversify your business.

Work in pairs. One of you plays the role of a business executive who is thinking of opening a factory to manufacture jeans. The other gives him/her advice. Using the expressions listed above, practise giving suitable advice.

*) promote
fashionable end
well made →suit*

*) cheaper
$40
first 6 months
after ↑*

*) big adv
campaign
↳ T.V. comm
↳ head gloms
↳ beoty
people
↳ poster
↓
bus, tube
bottles of
milk*

Problem

Gemma Fashions make clothing for young people between the ages of 18 and 25. The firm specializes in evening wear, producing the sort of clothes worn at discos, parties and clubs. Its merchandise is not expensive, though it is fashionable and well made.

Soon, the company will launch its new creation, a trouser suit. The suit costs $15 to manufacture, and its selling price has not yet been fixed. It is made of a lightweight material which looks—and feels—like silk. It should be ideal for the young woman who wants to look smart on a summer evening.

Unfortunately, fashionable clothing does not always sell well. Look what happened last year. The company brought out a lovely dress for summer wear. All Gemma's staff expected it to sell like hot cakes, but in fact few customers bought it.

Gemma does not want the same thing to happen with the trouser suit. She has contacted two advertising agencies and has asked each to consider how it would promote the suit. If one of them gives good advice and has interesting ideas, she will use that agency to carry out an advertising campaign for the new suit.

What do you think?

Gemma Kline and members of her management team meet two agencies, Pascoe Advertising and Lee Associates. They listen carefully to the advice and suggestions of each agency. After the meetings, Gemma and her team decide which agency will handle the campaign.

Instructions:

Divide into three groups: Gemma Fashions, Pascoe Advertising and Lee Associates. Read the instructions for your roles before you take part in the meetings.

Roles:

Gemma Fashions
You should meet Pascoe Advertising first, then Lee Associates. Listen to the advice and suggestions of each agency for promoting the trouser suit. Discuss each agency's ideas thoroughly. Then decide which one should handle the advertising campaign for the suit.

15

Pascoe Advertising/Lee Associates
Before you meet the management team from Gemma Fashions, you should think up ideas for promoting the trouser suit. The team will probably question you carefully about your suggestions, so these should be as detailed as possible.

Additional Discussion Topics

1. Here are some methods of advertising goods or services:

   newspaper/magazine/cinema/poster advertisements; direct-mail advertising; endorsements by famous people; demonstrations; trade exhibitions.

   Which is the *best* means for advertising these products/services?

   a) an expensive perfume
   b) a new type of tennis racket
   c) a new brand of orange
   d) an expensive car (e.g. a Rolls-Royce or Cadillac)
   e) the opening of a new restaurant
   f) an office cleaning service.

2. Describe an advertisement in your country which you particularly like. Are there any advertisements you dislike? If so, why?

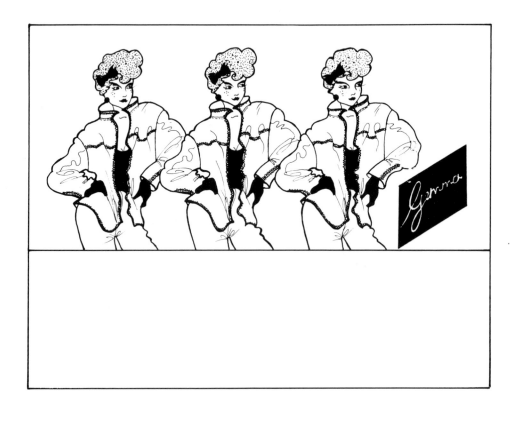

E Writing Exercise

Gemma Fashions have just launched their trouser suit. On the opposite page is a magazine advertisement for it, which shows a young woman modelling the style. Below the picture is a short text, called the advertising 'copy'. It gives information about the suit and advertises its qualities. It also aims to persuade readers to go out immediately and buy the new fashion.

Using about 100–140 words, write the text for the trouser suit advertisement.

F Listening Comprehension

Listen to the dialogue, noting down the important facts. Then complete the article about jeans by filling in the missing words (the letters of some words are given as a guide). If necessary, listen twice to the tape.

THE JEANS MARKET
How it all started

The first company to manufacture jeans was Levi Strauss. Over a century ago, its founder, Mr Levi Strauss, sold t*hese* . . c*lothes*. to people looking for gold. Then, he made jeans for them. The m*iner*. .s liked the trousers because they were very s.*trong*. . In the early days, jeans were really working clothes. Later on, they lost their w*orking* i*mage*. and became more fa*shionably* and s.*tyl*.*e*.ish.

In the 1960s, sales of jeans i*ncreas*ed rapidly. In fact, there was a jeans b*ooms*. . Because film stars wore them, they became p.*opular*. with young people. In the 1970s, people from all s.*ocial*. c.*lasse*.s wore them. Jeans became respectable! Even the President had a p.*anns*. . .

Levi Strauss is still the biggest jeans m*anufactur*. . . in the world. Some people are willing to pay a lot of money for designer jeans such as Gloria Vanderbilt and Vidal Sassoon b*rand* .s. These are heavily a*dvertis*.ed on television.

The total jeans market is worth . . . . . . *6 TM £*, but the market for high-fashion jeans is worth only about *7 M.M*. . . Many firms are c*ompe*ting for a share of that market. It's a c*ompet*tive field of business.

---

3 GOING PUBLIC

Companies sometimes obtain a stock exchange quotation. Why do they do it?

The London Stock Exchange.

Private and quoted companies are similar in one way: both have shareholders who own a part of the business. However, a private company cannot invite the general public to buy its shares and its shareholders cannot sell their shares unless the other members agree.

⁵ Anyone can buy the shares of a quoted company. They are freely bought and sold in a special market—the Stock Exchange. When a company wishes to be quoted, it applies to the Stock Exchange for a quotation, which is a statement of the share price. If the application is successful, the Stock Exchange deals in its shares and publishes their price each day.

¹⁰ There are three main reasons why companies obtain a quotation. First, many companies need to raise money to expand their businesses. For example, they want to build a bigger factory or produce a new range of goods. To finance this, they could try to get the money from a bank. But perhaps they have already borrowed heavily, so they do not want to increase their debt.

¹⁵ Secondly, there are companies which have been built up by their owners over the years. As the owner gets older, he does not want all his money to be tied up in the business. Therefore he sells part of the company to the public.

Finally, there is the type of business which started many years ago. It has now become a large company and its shares are spread among various members of a ²⁰ family. Some may have no interest in the company, while others have different ideas about how to run it. Shareholders disagree strongly, so it becomes difficult to run the company properly. In such a case, the only solution may be to obtain a quotation on the Stock Exchange.

There is one reason why the owners of a company may not wish to obtain a ²⁵ quotation. If the directors are the only shareholders—or have very large shareholdings—in their company, they may be getting substantial benefits from it. For example, the business may own things like the directors' houses, their cars and even their wives' cars. It pays perhaps for their petrol and holidays, which are business expenses. In this case, it may be better not to become a quoted company.

A Comprehension

1. What is the main difference between a *private* and *quoted* company?

2. How does a company obtain a stock exchange quotation?

3. Why do some companies prefer *not* to ask the bank to finance their expansion?

4. Explain the meaning of these phrases: (i) *tied up* (l. 16), (ii) *substantial benefits* (l. 26).

5. What problem can arise if several members of a family have shareholdings in a company?

6. Some directors do not want their companies to obtain a stock exchange quotation. Why?

B Vocabulary

1. Complete the passage below, using words from the box.

borrow	*capital*	*loan*
finance	*control*	*shares*
own	*debt*	
raise	*interest*	

If you . . . . . . a business, the time often comes when you wish to expand it.
To do so, you will need extra . . . . One way to get this is to . . . . . .
money from a bank. The bank makes a . . . . . . to you, but you pay . . . . . .
on the money it lends. Another way is to ask the bank for an overdraft. If it
agrees to give you one, you can then draw out money up to a certain limit.

You may, however, not want to owe money to the bank. You prefer not to
be in . . . . In that case, you could . . . . . . money by asking people to
invest in your business. In return for their investment, you would offer
them . . . . . . in your business. Finally, if you need a lot of money to
. . . . . . expansion, you may decide to go public. When you do this, you
usually lose some . . . . . . over your company.

2. Read the article, then do the exercises which follow it.

COMPANY NEWS

SHARE OFFER
BY KITCHEN MANUFACTURER

Next month, Zena plc, the well-known maker of kitchen appliances, will offer
for sale to the public two million shares. These will raise about £800,000 for
the company.

Zena supplies a wide range of equipment for the luxury kitchen market. It
specializes in high-quality cookers, freezers and refrigerators. The company
was founded in 1970. Its turnover has grown from £100,000 to £12 million.
Last year pre-tax profits were £1.6 million.

Chairman of the firm is Mr Gerald Knight. The board of directors—
average age 42—includes Mr Frank Bewley, sales director, and Mr Jasper
Levy, chief accountant.

Investors should jump at the chance to buy the shares. Zena has a good
profit record over the years. Its fixed assets are worth over £4 million.
Factories at Liverpool and Bristol (both freehold properties) are valued at £2.9
million. It also has plant and machinery worth £1 million. The company has
paid out excellent dividends since it obtained a quotation in 1976.

Zena are issuing new shares to finance their expansion into Europe. Next
year, they plan to set up a subsidiary in Zurich, Switzerland.

---

a) Which word or phrase in the text means . . . ?

  (i)   total sales;
  (ii) an executive who deals with financial matters;
  (iii) the amount of money a company has made up to the present;
  (iv) buildings owned for an unlimited time;
  (v) shares in the profits of a company—usually paid once or twice a year;
  (vi) to build, to establish.

b) What do these words and phrases mean?

> *specializes* (para. 2)
> *founded* (para. 2)
> *pre-tax profits* (para. 2)
> *fixed assets* (para. 4)
> *expansion* (para. 5)
> *subsidiary* (para. 5)

TATE & LYLE PLC
(Registered in England No. 76535)

1 for 4 Rights Issue

It was announced on 1st September, 1983 that the Directors are raising approximately £41 million by a 1 for 4 rights issue to holders of Ordinary Stock on the register at the close of business on 26th August, 1983 and to holders of Bearer Share Warrants.

Holders of Bearer Share Warrants who wish to claim their rights should note that relevant documents are available from The Secretary, Tate & Lyle PLC, Sugar Quay, Lower Thames Street, London EC3R 6DQ during usual business hours on presentation of Coupon number 54. Holders applying by post should supply their name and address. Payment is due by 27th September, 1983.

By Order of the Board,
C. P. McFie,
Secretary.

When a company wants to raise more money without borrowing it, new shares can be created and offered to existing shareholders. This is called a rights issue, because the shareholders are entitled to buy them as of right. The new shares are priced at about 20% less than the current market value.

C Language Practice

The company *has paid out* excellent dividends since it *obtained* a quotation in 1976.

Notice the two tenses used in this sentence.
The present perfect tense, 'has paid out', is used here to show that the action started in the past and continues in the present.
The past simple tense, 'obtained', is used here because the action happened at a fixed time in the past, 1976.

ZENA'S MAIN PRODUCTS 1983

Product	Brand name	Date of introduction	Volume of sales on introduction	Present volume of sales
Cookers	Verity	1971	£250,000	£360,000
	Windsor	1973	£190,000	£280,000
Refrigerators	Icicle	1972	£320,000	£200,000
	Arctic	1975	£260,000	£460,000
Freezers	Iceberg	1976	£200,000	£400,000
	Glacier	1978	£190,000	£290,000
Food processors	Genni	1977	£88,000	£188,000
	Miracle	1980	£122,000	£128,000

Exercises

At a meeting of Zena's shareholders the company chairman made this comment about the Verity cooker: 'Since the Verity cooker was first sold in 1971, sales have increased from £250,000 to £360,000.'

Make similar comments about the other products whose sales have gone up.

The company chairman said this about the Windsor cooker: 'When we introduced the Windsor cooker in 1973, sales were £190,000. Since then sales have gone up by £90,000.'

Make similar comments about the other products whose sales have gone up.

The company chairman said this about the Arctic refrigerator: 'The Arctic refrigerator has been on the market for eight years, and sales have gone up by £200,000.'

Make similar comments about the other products whose sales have gone up.

D Oral Work

Preparation   Opinions: asking for and giving opinions

Three directors of Nielsen plc are discussing the financial situation of their company. Kurt Nielsen is the firm's chairman; his brother Gunnar, managing director; Veronica, Gunnar's wife, is company secretary. Read or listen to the dialogue.

Kurt: In my opinion, things are looking very bad for us. Our turnover has gone up again this year but profits have dropped. What do you think, Gunnar?

Gunnar: I agree with you, Kurt, the situation's serious. In the last two years, our sales have increased, but profits have fallen—by more than 20% actually. I must say, I'm worried. How do you feel about it, Veronica?

Veronica: I'm not happy either, frankly. If you ask me, we can't expand any more in Britain. The market's saturated.

Kurt: Maybe you're right. We increased our market share by only 1% last year.

Veronica: Yes, and our costs went up by almost 25%. We spent a fortune on advertising and sales promotion.

Gunnar: That's because there's so much competition now. We are competing against big, low-cost European manufacturers—like the Germans and the Swiss. Each year, we have to cut our profit margins to keep up sales.

Kurt: You're right. These continental firms are really efficient. They have more modern machinery than us, and bigger markets, of course.

Veronica: And they offer a wider range of products. Their styles are different, exciting . . . . What on earth are we going to do about it?

Kurt: Look, I've thought carefully about our problems. One or two ideas have come to my mind. Let me tell you about them, then you can give me your views.

Practise these expressions

To give your opinion:

Examples:

In my opinion, we need to increase our product range.
I think (that) we should ask the bank for an overdraft.
If you ask me, our machinery is out-of-date.
In my view, this is not the time to apply for a quotation.

To ask for an opinion:

Examples:

What do you think?
What's your opinion/view?
How do you feel about this?

Useful expressions for agreeing/disagreeing:

Yes, I agree with you.
Yes, you're right.
Yes, I agree with you (entirely).

No, I don't agree (at all).
No, that's not true.
I disagree with you entirely.
I'm afraid I |*can't*| *agree with you.* (more polite)
         |*don't*|

Work in small groups. Using the discussion topics given below, practise giving your opinion and asking other members of the group for theirs.

1. To be successful in business, you must not be too honest.

2. A son/daughter should not work in his/her father's business.

Problem

G. and K. Nielsen plc is a family business. Kurt is chairman and his brother, Gunnar, managing director. They each own 30% of the shares. The remaining 40% of the share capital is divided equally between their four children. Kurt has one son. Gunnar and Veronica have a daughter and two sons, who all work for the company.

Until three years ago, Nielsen was doing well in the luxury kitchen market. Recently, profits have fallen while costs have risen. The company is now fighting hard to keep its market share.

Nielsen's problems are caused mainly by foreign manufacturers, who have been attracted by a market which is expanding by 15–20% a year. These firms, which have low costs, are selling luxury fitted kitchens at competitive prices (£6,000–£8,000 compared with Nielsen's £8,000–£10,000 price range). Competitors are also offering many different styles and product ranges.

Kurt is considering these ways of dealing with the problem:

1. *Expand into Europe*
   Nielsen could try to break into a European market, for example West Germany, France or Switzerland. People in those countries have high incomes, so they might not pay too much attention to price differences for fitted kitchens. They would probably like the high quality of Nielsen's products, and their English styles.

   The company could set up a small factory in one of the markets. To finance this expansion, Nielsen could obtain a stock exchange quotation. It could offer for sale about 45% of its shares. These would raise at least £2 million.

2. *Appoint a new person to run the company*
   Kurt is 60 years old, his brother is 52. Perhaps it is now time for a younger man to run the business? Should they bring in someone from outside the company and make that person managing director?

3. *Sell part of the business to a foreign company*
   A Danish furniture manufacturer has contacted Kurt. He wants to invest some of his firm's profits in a sound British firm. He has offered to buy 40–45% of Nielsen's shares for a good price (about £2.5 million). 'If we accept this offer,' thinks Kurt, 'we might be strong enough to compete against our European rivals.'

4. *Sell the whole business*
   They could, of course, sell out. They could then buy another business which was selling in a less competitive market.

What do you think?

You are the directors of the company. Consider the solutions to the problem. Discuss the advantages and disadvantages of each one. *Ask the other directors for their opinions and give your own views.* Finally, decide what action the company should take.

Note: If you wish, you may suggest a different solution to the problem.

Additional Discussion Topics

1. K. and G. Nielsen plc is a *family* business. What are the advantages and disadvantages of this type of business organization?

2. You have two friends. One wants to start a business in your country; the other wants to buy shares in a company. What kind of business and which company do you recommend? Why?

E Writing Exercise

You are the sales manager of Nielsen plc. You receive the following letter of complaint from Mrs A. Laidlaw. Reply to her letter, apologizing for the problems she has had with your products. Then tell her what the company will do to help.

---

10 Merton Road
London N17

10 November, 19--

K. and G. Nielsen plc
Moor Street
Manchester.

Dear Sir,

On 10 September, I ordered a complete fitted kitchen from your agent in our area. I chose the Prestige range. On 28 September, two men came from the shop and installed the equipment. When they had finished, I gave them a cheque as a final payment for the goods.

At first I was pleased with my new kitchen. But a few days later I noticed that the doors of the cabinets didn't shut properly, and that the handles had come off two drawers. Then, last Sunday I burned a leg of lamb because the clock on the cooker had stopped. Finally, two days ago I took a close look at the kitchen chairs. They were not the same type as I had ordered.

I have telephoned the shop many times, and often called in to see them. They also promised to send someone to inspect the kitchen, but no one has come to visit me yet. I am writing to you to ask if you can help me. I paid a lot of money for my Nielsen kitchen. Surely the shop should not treat me like this.

Yours faithfully

A. Laidlaw

Mrs A. Laidlaw

F Listening Comprehension

First, listen to the tape. Then listen again, and complete the sentences using information from the tape.

1. Most companies obtain a quotation because . . . .

2. The usual method of obtaining a quotation is to . . . .

3. If a firm decides to offer shares to the public, it usually contacts an . . . . . . or a . . . . . . These organizations will act for . . . .

4. Before helping a company, an issuing house collects information about it. For example, ...

5. A prospectus is . . . . In all prospectuses, there is an auditors' report. This is a . . . .

6. The prospectus is an important document because . . . .

7. Stockbrokers are very experienced, so they . . . .

8. Most companies use an underwriter because . . . .

9. In the example, the figures £70,000 and £30,000 refer to . . . .

10. For their work, the underwriters are paid a . . . .

4 DE BIJENKORF: FAMOUS DEPARTMENT STORE

These are some different types of sales outlet: (i) a department store (ii) a discount store (iii) a mail-order business (iv) a supermarket (v) a hypermarket (vi) an open market. BOOT SALE, JUMBLE SALE

In what ways are they different from each other? From which do you prefer to buy goods? Why?

De Bijenkorf, Dam Square, Amsterdam.

Most people have visited a department store. It is a large shop, divided into departments, each of which sells different lines of goods. The departments are run by managers, who are often called 'buyers', because their main duty is to purchase stock. The most famous stores offer a variety of beautiful and expensive
5 merchandise. When you go into them, you find a world of luxury and elegant living.

27

M W

If you visit Amsterdam, you can see the De Bijenkorf store. It is in Dam Square, right in the heart of the city. The store has been in business for over 70 years. It is part of a chain of five stores, which are located in major commercial centres.

The year 1976 was a turning point in the history of De Bijenkorf. At that time, the future for the stores seemed uncertain. Sales were falling, profits decreasing and fewer customers were bothering to make the journey through heavy traffic to shop in them.

De Bijenkorf were in trouble for several reasons. In the past 10 years, people had been moving away from the cities where the stores were situated. In Amsterdam, the population fell by 15%; in Rotterdam, it dropped by 17%. Most of those leaving were in the higher income groups.

The De Bijenkorf stores were also facing strong competition from discount houses, superstores and cash-and-carry businesses. These sold cheap or cut-price goods, though their service was often below standard.

Finally, De Bijenkorf were uncertain which section of the market they were aiming at. As a result, their image was not clear in the minds of the public. Sometimes, they had sales promotions to attract well-off buyers. At other times, they were offering price cuts on various items.

How could the management improve the stores' financial situation? To find the answer, they carried out a three-year study of their business. A team of research workers produced two important reports—the profitability analysis and the marketing analysis. The first showed which goods were actually making a profit; the second indicated those which were likely to be profitable in the future.

The information from the reports was very useful. It helped De Bijenkorf to decide which goods to continue selling, and which departments to keep open. The choice was not always easy. Some goods, such as toys, were not profitable, but they attracted customers, who then bought other things.

Naturally, the management made several changes as a result of the study. They got rid of some departments and expanded others. Then they created a new image for De Bijenkorf. They began to aim their sales strategy at people in higher income groups. In other words, the stores went up-market. In addition, the management spent a lot of money on renovating the interior of the buildings.

The changes were made to attract a special kind of customer—someone who liked good living. As the head of the stores said: 'We wanted a market where it is possible to express personality . . . where the type of goods you buy shows the kind of person you are.'

Language note

Line 19 *cash-and-carry*   A large shop where goods are sold at low prices if they are paid for at once and taken away by the buyer.

A Comprehension

1. What type of customer do big stores aim to attract?

2. Where are the De Bijenkorf stores situated? What problem have they had because of their location?

3. Why did the management of De Bijenkorf decide to make a careful study of their stores?

4. What did the management learn from their study?

5. Explain the meaning of these phrases:

   elegant living (l. 5)
   uncertain which section of the market they were aiming at (l. 21)
   sales promotions (l. 23)
   sales strategy (l. 36)
   went up-market (l. 37)

6. What kind of image did De Bijenkorf have (a) before 1976 and (b) after the three-year study had been carried out?

B Vocabulary

1. Complete this table.

Verb	Noun	Adjective
shop	SHOPPER/SHOPPING	SHOPPING
COMPETE	competition	*COMPETITIVE*
expand	*EXPANSION*	*EXPANDING*
sell	*SALES/SELLER*	*SELLING*
PROMOTE	*PROMOTION*	promotional
FINANCE	*FINANCE*	financial
ANALYSE	analysis	*ANALYSIS/ANALYTICAL*
choose	*CHOICE*	*CHOOSING*
VARY	*VARIETY*	various
MARKET	market /*MARKETING*	*MARKETING/MARKET/MARKETABLE*
buy	*BUYER/BUY*	*BUYING*
manage	*MANAGER/MANAGEMENT*	*MANAGING/MANAGEABLE*
inform	*INFORMER/INFORMATION*	*INFORMATIVE*
STANDARDIZE	standard	*STANDARD*

2. Complete the passage using words from the list below.

~~costs~~	~~expenditure~~	renovation	~~sales~~
deliveries	~~facilities~~	research	~~shop~~
~~display~~	~~overheads~~	retailer	shopping
~~expense~~	~~performance~~	~~retailing~~	~~stock~~

De Bijenkorf is not the only big *retailer* which has problems. Selfridges, the London department store, has also had to make changes in order to stay profitable. The store is situated in Oxford Street, which has always been the 'Mecca' of *retailing*, and one of the most famous *shopping* areas in the world.

   At the end of the 1970s, Selfridges faced several problems. Like most stores, its *overheads* such as heating, lighting, local taxes, etc., had risen sharply. In addition, its operating *costs* generally were too high. When a new boss, Mr Roy Stevens, took over in 1979, he immediately looked for new ways of reducing *expenses*. Starting with the merchandise, he reviewed the product ranges, and slow-moving goods were taken off the shelves. On the supply side, he made sure that *deliveries* from manufacturers were carefully planned, so that *stock* levels were kept low. At the same time, the number of personnel was reduced—cuts being made in both *sales* and administrative staff.

The management wanted Selfridges to be a pleasant place to *shop* in. Therefore, they carried out a programme of *renovation*, making the store brighter and cleaner. Also, they improved the *facilities* of the building. Each floor has its own *display* team. They compete against each other to show off goods attractively.

Managers check the sales *performance* of each department regularly—trading figures are sent to key departments daily. The store's *expenditure* on advertising and promotion is large—over £2 million a year. Finally, Selfridges is doing a lot of *research* to find out more about its customers.

C Language Practice

To find the answer, De Bijenkorf carried out a three-year study.
The part of the sentence in italics tells us why they carried out a three-year study. Why were the changes made at De Bijenkorf? To attract a special kind of customer.

When John Hudson became the new boss at Millhurst's department store, he sent this note to all the heads of department.

Millhurst's Department Store
11 London Street   Hamsville   Wessex
Tel: 0111 011011   Telex: 009009

Dear Colleague,
As you are well aware, this store must improve profitability. I suggest there are several things we can do to achieve this. These are as follows:
Attract customers from a higher income group to the store.
Give the store a new up-to-date image.
Improve our window displays.
Get more young customers into the store.
Identify which goods are slow moving.
Keep stock levels lower.
Decide which kinds of department to set up and what services to introduce.
Decide which slow-moving goods to go on selling.
Work out which evening to stay open late.

Please bring along suggestions to the meeting in my office at 3 o'clock next Tuesday.
John Hudson
Managing Director.

Here are the notes Sue Cook, one of the heads of department, took to the meeting.

Suggestions about how to improve profitability:
Introduce a new top-quality range of young people's wear.
Hire Bell and Bell, the famous shop designers.
Send someone on a fact-finding tour of successful stores.
Make sure deliveries from manufacturers are carefully planned.
Discover when people eat out in the evenings.
Carry out a very careful stock review.
Find out which goods attract people into the store.
Stock lines of top-quality goods.
Get some students straight from art school.

Exercise 1

Match Sue Cook's suggestions with the aims Mr Hudson wants to achieve. Then make sentences as in the example.

Example:

They should introduce a new top-quality range of young people's wear to get more young customers into the store.

Exercise 2 (Work in pairs)

Now ask and answer questions like this:

A: Why did she suggest they introduced a new top-quality range of young people's wear?

B: To get more young customers into the store.

D Oral Work

Preparation   Making deductions

Each year, department stores lose money because customers or members of staff steal goods. This conversation is about Tom, a management trainee in a large store. Read or listen to the dialogue.

Security manager: I've just had a long talk with Smith, Tom's departmental manager. I'm afraid Tom did steal those rings. He must have taken them first thing in the morning because Smith noticed they were missing at 11 o'clock when he brought out a tray to serve a customer.

Personnel director: I can't believe it. There must be some mistake.

General manager: I must say, it's a surprise to me, but I don't think Smith would make a mistake about a matter like this. I'd better see them both and we'll call in the police. We can't have thieves behind our counters. We must make an example of Tom, don't you think?

Personnel director: Yes, but we don't want to make an example of ourselves. After all, we must have checked his background twice over. There must be some reason for this that we don't know.

Security manager: Could I make a suggestion?

General manager: Go ahead.

Security manager: Let Sheila talk to him first. Don't forget, he's a potential manager. We spent a lot of money training him. There may be more to this than we know.

General manager: I suppose you're right. OK then, Sheila, you have a talk with him. But he's got to have a good excuse for this.

Practise these expressions

To make deductions:

Examples:

Tom must have a good reason for stealing the rings.
The jewellery department must be one of our most profitable businesses.
Smith must have been surprised when he saw the jewellery was missing.
Tom must have provided references when he applied to join the store.

Comment on these situations by *making deductions*.

Example: It is 6 o'clock in the evening. A bell is ringing loudly throughout the store.
Comment: *Then it must be closing time.*

1. The store has been packed with customers every day this week.

2. Jennifer has received two big wage increases recently.

3. During a recent stock-taking, it was discovered that £20,000 worth of goods had 'disappeared'.

4. When the manager arrived at the store this morning, the burglar alarm was ringing.

5. During the past year, more than 30% of the sales staff have given in their notice.

6. Peter joined the store 10 years ago as a clerk in the accounts department. He is now managing director.

Problem

Tom has been with the department store for two years. As a management trainee, he has spent a lot of time working in the different departments of the organization. For the past month, he has been helping out in the jewellery and giftware department. As part of his training programme, he has also attended a number of seminars on management.

Tom is considered to be a promising employee who has the makings of a first-class manager. He is 18 years old.

When the management found out that Tom had taken some rings from the jewellery department, they were shocked. However, they decided to ask the personnel manager, Sheila, to see Tom and get his story. This is the story that Tom told her.

Tom and his sister live with their 55-year-old mother. The family has always been poor. The father died when the children were very young. Their mother has earned a living by working as a waitress and doing office-cleaning jobs. Naturally, she was delighted when Tom got such a good job at the store. Life became a little easier for them all.

But a few months ago Tom's mother developed a painful cyst on her left leg. At times she could hardly walk. The operation she required was not serious, but she was told that it might be weeks before she could get a place in hospital.

Time went by. Tom could not bear to see his mother in such pain. He telephoned the doctor. 'How much will the operation cost if it's done privately?' he asked. 'About £500' was the answer.

Tom couldn't raise so much money. Then a young friend who worked on a newspaper suggested this strange scheme. Tom should 'borrow' some jewellery from the departmental stock but he must keep it safe and not sell it. When the management discovered that the jewellery was missing, Tom should tell them the whole story. After that, his friend could write a newspaper article about Tom. It would be about a boy tempted to steal to pay for his mother's operation, but unable to carry out the crime. The friend assured Tom that the story would raise public sympathy, and probably enough money to pay for his mother's operation.

The personnel manager reported all this to her management colleagues.

What do you think?

The general manager calls a meeting to discuss this matter. The following staff are present: general manager, company lawyer, personnel director, security manager, head of the jewellery department.

Work in groups of five. Each person plays one of the roles described below. The purpose of the meeting is to discuss the problem thoroughly, then to agree on a suitable course of action.

Roles:

General manager
You are the leader of the discussion. This could be a tricky meeting. You might be persuaded by the others. You think that Tom should be sacked because he is not reliable enough to make a good manager. He should have been more sensible and come to management to present his problem and ask for a loan of the money. He should not have listened to his friend's advice, which you think is nonsense.

Personnel director
You are completely convinced by Tom's story. You are sure he is an honest

person. He has shown this by being unable to go through with the crime. The training programme has already cost the store more than the £500 which is at stake. If Tom leaves, that money will be wasted. He should be given another chance.

Company lawyer
You advise the general manager not to sack Tom. If the store dismisses Tom, there will be an even more sensational newspaper story resulting in bad publicity for the store. The general manager should see Tom, point out the mistake he has made, tell him to make sure his friend does not print the story, and offer to lend him the money for his mother's operation.

Security manager
You agree with the general manager and want to sack Tom. The store will never be able to trust him again. Therefore, he can never become a manager. He has shown no judgement in this matter. There are many other young people looking for jobs. It will not be difficult to replace Tom.

Head of the jewellery department
Tom should be given another chance. He is an excellent worker; one of the best trainees you have ever had. While Tom was working in your department, he often talked about his mother. He was very worried about her health. In your opinion the store should lend Tom the money for his mother's operation and they should allow the whole story to be printed in the newspaper. It would be good publicity for the store. £500 is not a lot of money—the store spends much more than that on publicity each week. Perhaps the store could even pay for the entire cost of Tom's mother's operation.

E Writing Exercise

You are the owner of a security services firm. One day, you listen to a radio programme called *Business in Focus*. The manager of Goodies Department Store is being interviewed. He complains that his business is losing a lot of money because of employee theft and shoplifting.[1]

Write to the manager of the store. Introduce yourself and your firm. Give the manager details of the services your company can offer (if you wish, use the vocabulary listed below). Say how much these services cost. Finally, suggest that you meet him soon to discuss the matter further.

Vocabulary

fire/burglar alarm	*closed-circuit television*
alarm system	*two-way mirrors*
(uniformed) security guards	*to provide*
(highly trained) store detectives	*to instal*
two-way radio	*cheap/competitive rates*

[1] *Shoplifting* Customers stealing goods from a shop.

F Listening Comprehension

1. Listen to the dialogue. As you do so, note down the sales figures for each month. Then complete the chart so that it gives a picture of the store's wine sales for the whole year.

2. Listen to the dialogue again. Note all the reasons for the variations in the figures. Then, working in pairs, play the roles of John and Vicky. Talk about the figures, using the chart as a guide.

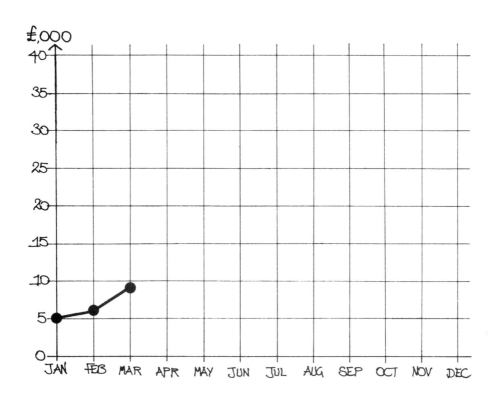

5 BIG IS BEAUTIFUL

What qualities do you need to become a millionaire? Which millionaire, if any, do you particularly admire or dislike?

The River Amazon.

The Amazon basin is a huge area in Brazil. It has always attracted businessmen because it has valuable resources such as rubber, cocoa, coffee, timber and minerals. However, it is not easy to make money by starting an enterprise there. If you wish to succeed in the Amazon, the Brazilians say, 'you must believe in the
5 country—and you must be young'.

Rich men have poured money into the region and gone away empty-handed. In the 1930s Henry Ford lost a lot of money trying to grow rubber near the River Tapajos. Thirty years later another American billionaire, Mr Daniel Ludwig,

came to Brazil with a very ambitious project. He wanted to build an enormous
pulp factory on the Jari river in the Amazon.

Pulp is made by softening and crushing wood. It is used to produce paper. In the
1950s Mr Ludwig was certain that the demand for this material was going to
increase. He thought there would be a worldwide shortage of pulp and paper by
the 1980s. So in 1967 he bought four million acres of Brazilian forest and began
organizing his pulp business.

Actually, this business was only part of the Jari river project. Mr Ludwig had
plans to make a hydro-electric dam which would supply power for an aluminium
factory. And there would be other enterprises producing paper, meat, rice, cheese
and tropical fruit.

He knew his project was risky, but he was used to taking risks. Earlier in his life
he had made a fortune in ship-building because he had been one of the first to build
giant oil tankers. At Jari he was also ahead of everyone else. He was the first to use
floating factories. Two of these plants were brought by sea all the way from Japan
to Brazil. Nowadays floating factories can be found all over the world.

Mr Ludwig spent 14 years trying to realize his dream. During that time he
invested over $1 billion in his project. However, by 1981 he had not made a penny
profit from the enterprise, so he decided to sell it to a group of Brazilian
businessmen.

Why did he fail? Without doubt his biggest mistake was to be wrong about the
pulp market. There was no world shortage of pulp. In the past 20 years, supplies
have been plentiful and demand weak. Because of this, the company was not able
to raise its prices.

In addition, some people say the project was badly managed. Mr Ludwig made
all the important decisions from his office in New York, only visiting Jari from
time to time. His relations with the Brazilian government were poor as well. There
was a big dispute about who should pay for the roads, railway and social services at
Jari.

While he was selling the Jari enterprise, Mr Ludwig—at the age of 84—was
planning other projects. He was interested in buying one million acres of land in
Paraguay to grow grain. Also, he was thinking of shipping coal from a floating
terminal off America's east coast.

A Comprehension

1. What does the title of the text mean? Do you think it is a suitable title? If
   so, why?

2. Explain why Mr Ludwig's plans were ambitious?

3. What is pulp? Of which substance is it the raw material?

4. What do we know about Mr Ludwig's previous business experience?

5. What are some of his qualities? Does he have any weaknesses?

6. Why did Mr Ludwig's dreams *not* come true?

B Vocabulary

1. Which word or phrase in the text means . . . ?

    a) the wealth of a country—its raw materials, goods, etc. (para. 1);

    b) an enterprise requiring a big investment and whose success is uncertain (para. 2);

    c) insufficient supplies (para. 3);

    d) a measure of area (para. 3);

    e) a wall to keep back water (para. 4);

    f) large ships for transporting fuel (para. 5);

    g) available in large quantities (para. 7);

    h) seeds used to grow wheat and other food plants (para. 9).

2. Write down *two* other words which mean the same as:

    huge (l. 1)   . . . .
    area (l. 1)   . . . .
    project (l. 9)   . . . .
    produce (l. 11)   . . . .
    enterprise (l. 18) . . . .
    dispute (l. 36)   . . . .

3. Complete these sentences using the words in italics.

crops	*land*	*power*	*soil*
develop	*mineral*	*regions*	
incentives	*policy*	*schemes*	

    a) Some . . . . . . of the Amazon basin have not been developed at all.

    b) Much of the . . . . . . in the region is poor and nothing will grow there.

    c) The government is considering how to . . . . . . the mineral region of Carajás.

    d) Most of the . . . . . . is cheap to buy, but markets are far away.

    e) The present government has a . . . . . . of encouraging people to live in the Amazon.

    f) In Rondonia, they are growing . . . . . . such as rubber, cocoa and coffee.

    g) The Minister of Development has thought up a number of . . . . . . to attract businessmen to this part of Brazil.

    h) The Amazon Development Agency, SUDAM, has offered tax . . . . . . so that people will set up cattle farms there.

    i) Water . . . . . . is a cheap source of energy.

    j) Bauxite is the . . . . . . used to produce aluminium.

C Language Practice

Earlier in his life he *had made* a fortune in ship-building.

The *past perfect tense* is used here to make it clear that he made the fortune before he went to Jari.

However, by 1981 he *had not made* a penny profit.
The past perfect tense is used here to show that he did not make a penny profit *up until* 1981.

The Strand Paper Group

The paper-making industry has been badly affected by the world economic situation. The Strand Paper Group closed many of its plants, stopped production of several kinds of paper and lost several contracts before it was bought by Collbrook Paper in 1982. This is a summary of what happened to Strand before it was sold.

1978	Closure of Fort Bean plant—400 men lost their jobs. Stopped production of photographic paper—100 jobs lost. Loss of contract to supply paper for tickets to Euroair.
1979	Production reduced at the Fulton and Maddox plants—300 jobs lost. Loss of contract to supply Harpers' supermarkets with price tickets. Loss of contract to supply paper to British TV.
1980	Closure of Fulton plant—250 jobs lost. Stopped production of wallpaper—200 jobs lost. Loss of contract to supply Hamilton Hotels with paper serviettes.
1981	Closure of Maddox plant—180 jobs lost. Stopped production of gift wrapping paper—100 jobs lost. Stopped production of paper serviettes—100 jobs lost.

Here are some comments which appeared in an article about the sale of the Strand Paper Group:

'When they lost the Harpers' contract they had already lost the Euroair contract.'

'When they reduced production at the Fulton and Maddox plants they had already closed the Fort Bean plant.'

'By the beginning of 1979, 500 men had lost their jobs.'

'When they closed the Fulton plant they had already reduced production at the Fulton and Maddox plants.'

'When they lost the contract to supply Hamilton Hotels with paper serviettes they had already lost the Harpers and British TV contracts.'

'By the beginning of 1980 300 men had lost their jobs.'

'When they closed the Maddox plant they had already closed the Fulton plant.'

'By the beginning of 1981, 450 men had lost their jobs.'

Exercise 1

Make similar comments comparing the situations in 1979 and 1980, and 1980 and 1981.

Exercise 2

Find out:

1. The number of men who had lost their jobs when the group was sold.

2. Which contracts they had lost when the group was bought in 1982.

3. What they had stopped producing when Collbrook bought the group.

4. Which plants the group had closed down when Collbrook acquired the group.

D Oral Work

Preparation   Making conditions

The American multi-millionaire, Jason Roebuck, is planning a new project. He wants to develop the mineral region of Carajás, in the Amazon basin. He is talking to two friends, Paula and Magnus. Read or listen to the dialogue.

Jason: Well, you've had a chance now to look at the reports and studies of the Carajás region. You know what I think. The area's got enormous potential, but we'll have to move fast. Other people are interested in developing it.

Magnus: You've certainly convinced me, Jason. I'll put money in the project if we can make a good deal with the Brazilians. How about you, Paula?

Paula: I'm very impressed by the studies. I never knew Carajás was so rich in minerals.

Jason: It's got everything—gold, bauxite, copper, nickel and tin—that's why the project's so interesting.

Paula: It's interesting, all right. And I'm willing to invest in it. At least, providing the Brazilian government help us.

Jason: That's important, I agree. It's not worth starting the project unless they back us up. There'll be plenty of problems—not just financial ones. The government will be able to solve most of them.

Magnus: When do you think we should go to Carajás, Jason?

Jason: Mmm . . . in about six weeks' time, perhaps?

Magnus: That would be OK, as long as we prepare for the visit right away.

Jason: Yes, the trip will need careful planning.

Paula: There's one thing I'd like to say, Jason. As you know, I'm used to dealing with South Americans . . .

Jason: Yes?

Paula: In my opinion, we should be able to make a deal with the Brazilians—but we must show them that we know what we want.

Practise these expressions

To make conditions:

Examples:

If we can mine gold and bauxite, we'll make a lot of money.
We'll be successful providing we plan the project carefully.
It's not worth taking the risk unless we can make a big profit.

A group of foreign businessmen are planning to set up a mining project in the Amazon region. Using the sentence openings given below, make comments about the project.

1. The Brazilians will approve our project providing . . . .

2. It's not worth mining tin unless . . . .

3. We'll make a fortune as long as . . . .

4. The government will pay for roads and a hospital, but only if . . . .

5. We'll employ local workers but they must . . . .

6. The project should break even after five years if . . . .

Now make other similar comments.

Problem

The Carajás region is south of the River Amazon. It contains large amounts of iron ore, as well as other minerals such as gold, nickel, copper and bauxite.

The government want to develop the area, but to develop the mines, metal-making industry and other projects will cost about $60 billion. $22 billion of that money will be needed for essential services—roads, railways, housing, hospitals, etc.

Jason Roebuck's plan is simple. He wants to lead a group of American investors who will mine *some* of the minerals in Carajás.

What do you think?

Jason Roebuck is now in Brazilia (the capital of Brazil). He is accompanied by several business partners. This afternoon, he will meet some Brazilian officials, including the ministers of trade, planning and Amazon development.

The Americans will talk about their project to these officials. At the end of the meeting, both groups will try to reach some kind of agreement.

Instructions:

Work in two groups. You play the part of an American investor or Brazilian official. The Minister of Trade leads the discussion. Read the notes for your role before the meeting begins.

Roles:

American investors

You plan to invest $20 million in the project. You wish to mine these minerals: gold, bauxite, nickel and tin. You are not interested in iron ore because world demand for it is weak. If you set up the project, you intend to employ American managers—they are highly trained and experienced. You are willing to work with a local Brazilian firm provided it does not share more than 25% of the project's profits. If possible, you should persuade the Brazilians that *they* must pay for services such as roads, railways, hospitals, etc. Your leader, Jason Roebuck, plans to visit Carajás briefly two or three times a year. A young American will be in charge of the project. He will phone or telex Roebuck if problems arise.

Brazilian officials

Be careful! You know very little about these American investors. Suggest that they start by mining iron ore, bauxite and nickel. A few years later, you *may* let them mine gold as well. Try to persuade the Americans to accept some (or all) of these conditions: (i) they must invest at least $2 billion in iron ore mines; (ii) they should pay $4 billion towards the cost of essential services (roads, railways, etc.); (iii) half the project managers should be Brazilians; (iv) a Brazilian firm should provide 50% of the capital and share 50% of the profits; (v) Jason Roebuck must spend at least three months each year in Carajás because he will have to approve all major decisions.

Additional Discussion Topics

1. Are there any regions in your country which need developing? If so, what is your government doing to help their development?

2. If you were very rich, what type of project would you like to carry out?

E Writing Exercise

After meeting the Brazilians, Jason Roebuck sends a telex to his friend, Abe Johnston. Abe is interested in investing in the project but has been unable to go with Jason to Brazilia. In the telex, Jason tells his friend about the meeting with the Brazilian officials, and gives details of any agreement they may have reached.

Here is the beginning of the telex.[1] You must now complete it.

---

[1] Telexes are less expensive to send than cables or telegrams, but they cost more to send than letters. Therefore, the sender of a telex tries to be as brief as possible. These are some well-known abbreviations (short forms) which can be used in telexes: Soonest = as soon as possible; OK = agreed/do you agree?; RPT = I repeat; SVP = please.

```
63888   JOHNSTON
43781   ROEBUCK HOTEL MAJESTA BRAZILIA

12.8.83

TODAY, WE MET THE BRAZILIAN OFFICIALS AND HAD A LONG DISCUSSION.
WE EXPLAINED OUR PLANS FOR CARAJAS .......   ........  ........
```

F Listening Comprehension

First, listen to the dialogue. Then, listen again and answer the questions.

1. Why is Karen's boss going to be pleased with her?
2. What does her boss think of the articles she writes?
3. Why has it been difficult for Mr Ludwig to sell his company?
4. How did the company do last year?
5. Who is Mr Augustino Antunes?
6. What do we learn about his business activities in the Amazon?
7. What is Mr Antunes planning to do?
8. Who will be his business partners?
9. Will Mr Ludwig lose all his money in the pulp project?
10. What does Karen mean when she says: 'Good luck to them'?

6 THE JAPANESE WORKER

Is it better to stay with one firm throughout your working life or to change firms from time to time?

Early morning workout for the Mabushita Electric Company workers.

- In Japan, there is a close relationship between the worker and his company.
- Employees work hard and do hours of unpaid overtime to make their firms more efficient. If necessary, they give up weekends with the family to go on business
- trips. They are loyal to their organizations and totally involved with them. For
5 example, many of them live in company houses, their friends are people they work with, and in their spare time they do sports and other activities organized by their employers.

The system of lifetime employment creates a strong link between the enterprise and its workforce. It covers about 35% of the working population. Generally,

10 when a person joins a firm after leaving high school or university, he expects to stay with that firm until he retires. He has a secure job for life. Therefore, he will not be laid off if the company no longer needs him because there is no work. Instead, it will retrain him for another position.

The pay of a worker depends on his seniority, that is to say, on the years he has
15 been with the firm. The longer he stays there, the higher his salary will be. When he is 30 or 40 years old, therefore, he cannot afford to change jobs. If he did move, he would also lose valuable fringe benefits. Promotion depends on seniority as well. Japanese managers are rarely very young, and chief executives are at least 60, and very often 70 years old.

20 The Japanese have a special way of making decisions. They call it the consensus system. This is how it works. When a firm is thinking of taking a certain action, it encourages workers at all levels to discuss the proposal and give their opinions. The purpose is to reach consensus (general agreement). As soon as everyone agrees on the right course of action, the decision is taken.

25 Because of this method, a group of workers, rather than one person, is responsible for company policies. One advantage of this is that decisions come from a mixture of experience from the top, the middle and the bottom of an enterprise. Another advantage is that junior staff frequently suggest ideas for change. A disadvantage, perhaps, is that decision-making can be slow.

WHEN YOU WORK FOR A COMPANY, YOU BECOME PART OF IT

A Comprehension

1. What are the main qualities of Japanese workers?

2. When business conditions are bad, a Japanese worker is probably more secure than a European one. Why?

3. Why do people not change jobs very frequently in Japan?

4. How do they make decisions in Japanese companies?

5. What are the advantages and disadvantages of: (i) lifetime employment, (ii) payment by seniority, (iii) promotion by seniority, (iv) consensus decision-making?

B Vocabulary

1. Match the words to the meanings.

a) overtime	(i)	plans, courses of action
b) workforce	(ii)	an organization/business firm
c) laid off	(iii)	to give up work at a certain age
d) seniority	(iv)	all the employees in a firm
e) fringe benefits	(v)	getting a higher position
f) policies	(vi)	advantages offered by a company, besides wages
g) enterprise		or salary
h) promotion	(vii)	sent away because no work is available
i) retrain	(viii)	work done in addition to normal working hours
j) retire	(ix)	length of service
	(x)	teach someone to do a new job

45

2. The words in the box are connected with employment. Find out what they mean, then use some of them to complete the passages below. (*Note:* You must change the forms of some words.)

apply	*interview*	*train*
application	*interviewer*	*training*
applicant		*trainee*
	appoint	
employ	*appointment*	*promote*
employer		*promotion*
employee	*dismiss (formal)*	
	fire (informal)	*resign*
	sack (informal)	

a) When a firm wants to fill a vacancy, it puts an advertisement in a newspaper. Several people usually . . . . . . for the position. After . . . . . . the applicants, the firm selects the most suitable person for the job. He or she is then . . . . . . to the position and becomes an . . . . . . of the company.

b) Sometimes, a firm has to . . . . . . people who have no special skills or experience. It must, therefore, ... them to do their job. Workers who are learning a job are called . . . . Later on, when they are very experienced, they may be offered a more responsible position. Employees who are . . . . . . generally receive a pay increase.

c) No company likes to lose staff. However, if an employee breaks the rules, he or she may be . . . . Of course, there are always staff who want to leave for various reasons. To do this, they . . . . . . from their job and give their . . . . . . a certain period of notice.

C Language Practice

The Japanese worker expects to stay with the company *until he retires.*
When the Japanese worker is forty, he cannot afford to leave. He joins the company *after he has left school.*
    Notice that the verbs in the time clauses are not in the future tense.

Read the following extract from a paper-making group's recruiting leaflet.

> . . . we train our future managers as thoroughly as possibly. The initial training consists of seven stages:
>
> 1. A two-week induction course.
>
> 2. Six weeks' training in a paper-making unit.
>
> 3. A two-week introduction to the industry's technology.
>
> 4. Six weeks' experience in a paper-coating unit.
>
> 5. A one-week communications course.
>
> 6. Six weeks' specialized training for your first appointment.
>
> 7. One week's lectures on the group's structure and the inter-relations of its operations.

Salary progression and benefits
The trainee scheme will take you to a salary in the range of
£8,000–£8,500 within two years. You can join the group's pension
scheme after six months. The holiday entitlement is 20 days per annum
after nine months.

Exercise 1

The group's recruiting officer visits a university where he gives a talk to
students who are interested in joining the group.
   'When a management trainee starts with the group he receives 24 weeks'
initial training.'
   Continue the recruiting officer's description of the training, using the
outlines below.

a) *When/he/join/attend . . .*

b) *Once/finish/induction course/get . . .*

c) *As soon as/complete/ . . . /he/get . . .*

d) *When/finish/ . . . /have/ . . .*

e) *Once/complete/ . . . /attend . . .*

f) *When/leave/ . . . /get . . .*

Exercise 2

Example:
When does he get six weeks' specialized training?
After *he has gone* on a one-week communications course.

Find out:

1. When he learns about the group's structure.

2. When he earns about £8,000.

3. When he joins the group's pension scheme.

4. When he can have his first holiday.

D Oral Work

Preparation   Agreeing/doubting

*Toshi Kato is head of a Japanese electronics firm. The firm has just built a new
factory in England which will make television sets. It will go into production in a
few weeks' time. Toshi is talking to two of the managers, Jerry and Anita. Read or
listen to the dialogue.*

Toshi: If we want to succeed in the European market, we've got to work hard.
           And also work as a team. It's very important—teamwork. Don't forget,
           we'll have to produce half a million sets in the next year.

Jerry: Half a million? Mmm . . . . I don't know about that. It's a high target, isn't it?

Anita: I agree with you, Jerry. I mean . . . our workers are good, but they're not as productive as the Japanese.

Toshi: Maybe, but they could be. I've been thinking a lot about the personnel lately. How to make them work harder . . . .

Anita:
Jerry: Yes?

Toshi: Well, I think we could use some of our Japanese methods here in the factory. They've been very successful in our country.

Jerry: In Japan, maybe, but here in England . . . I have my doubts somehow.

Anita: Oh, I don't know, Jerry. Some new methods might be worth trying.

Jerry: Perhaps. What exactly do you have in mind, Toshi?

Toshi: Well, there are many things we could do. In my country, we have physical exercises each day for half an hour. They're good for workers—they keep you fit. We could do something like that here.

Jerry: I don't think they'd be very popular somehow. If you ask me, everybody would go on strike.

Anita: I think you're right, Jerry. English people just wouldn't like that sort of thing.

Practise these expressions

To agree with someone:

Examples:

I agree with you (completely/entirely).
I think you're right.
That's (absolutely) true.
I couldn't agree with you more.

To show doubt:

Examples:

Mmm, I don't know about that.
I have my doubts somehow.
Mmm, maybe.
Do you really think so?

Below, speaker A is talking about Japan and its people. Show whether you agree with him or have doubts by making appropriate comments in the spaces provided:

Example:

    A: The Japanese make the best pocket calculators in the world.
      I couldn't agree with you more.

1. A: The best hi-fi sets come from Japan.
   . . . . . .

2. A: The Japanese work too hard.
   . . . . . .

3. A: The prices of Japanese products are low because Japanese workers do not earn high wages.
   . . . . . .

4. A: Japanese cars offer the best value for money in the world.
   . . . . . .

5. A: In manufacturing, the Japanese prefer to copy rather than to create.
   . . . . . .

Now, working in pairs, make up similar conversations.

Problem

Toshi Kato wants the English workers to be as efficient as possible. Therefore, he would like to introduce some Japanese methods into the new factory. He makes these suggestions to a group of the factory's managers:

All workers in the factory (including managers) should wear blue uniforms.

Each morning before work, all employees should sing a company song; at 11 o'clock every day, they should do physical exercises to keep fit.

No worker should be allowed to go on strike. Anyone refusing to work should be dismissed.

Once a week, employees should stay on after work to discuss production problems. No overtime payment would be made for such duties.

All members of staff, including top managers, should eat together in the company cafeteria.

What do you think?

Instructions:

One of you is Toshi Kato, who leads the discussion. The others play the roles of the factory's managers. You should consider Toshi's suggestions, and either agree with him or express your doubts. The purpose of the meeting is to decide which proposals to put into practice in the factory.

Additional Discussion Topics

1. Why are the Japanese so successful in overseas markets?

2. Should foreign governments allow Japanese companies to build factories in their countries?

E Writing Exercise

Two business people meet by chance in a hotel. One of them is from Japan, the other from another country. They get into conversation and begin to compare working conditions in their countries. They discuss these subjects: job security; wages/salaries; promotion; decision-making; fringe benefits.

Write the dialogue that takes place between these two people.

F Listening Comprehension

First, listen to the dialogue. Then listen again, completing the notes made by Miss Walker during the interview.

Interview with Mr Toshi Kato

1. In Mr Kato's company, they offer lifetime employment to . . . .

2. There is no job security for . . . .

3. Since 1955 . . . .

4. 1974 was a very difficult time because . . . .

5. Employees without work did other things, for example . . . .

6. The workers are well educated. Most of them . . . .

7. The factory needs educated workers because . . . .

8. The reason why the company makes high-quality products: '. . . . .', Mr Kato says!

7 AMERICAN UNIONS

What are the advantages of being in a union? Are there any disadvantages?

An American worker displays his union membership card. His union is the United Cannery, Agricultural, Packing and Allied Workers of America.

In the United States, the power of the unions is decreasing. There are clear signs that they are losing their hold on workers.

Nowadays, only 20% of the workforce are in a union. In 1955, however, 34% of workers were members. The unions are also having trouble getting new members.
5 They are winning only 45% of the elections by which workers decide whether they want to become union members.

The battle between management and labour can be hard, especially in the southern states of the United States. When the south was still mainly a rural society, the unions did not pay much attention to it. But, in the past 10 years, many companies have moved there. During that time, the northern states—where unions are strong—have lost over one million jobs; employees have moved to the non-union south.

Southern employers do not welcome the unions. They are suspicious of them and think that they can do without them. Every southern state has a right-to-work law. This forbids compulsory union membership. In other words, when a worker joins a company he or she does not have to become a union member.

Because they dislike unions, southern businessmen often try to keep them outside their factory gates. Sometimes, the fight can be hard and bitter. One union had to wait 17 years, and spend millions of dollars in the law courts, before it could recruit workers inside a textile factory.

Some Americans believe that unions will disappear from their society. They say that more and more companies will develop good personnel policies, so that unions will be unnecessary. To prove their point they give examples of companies in the north which have excellent working conditions.

These firms have stayed non-union by paying above-average wages and offering first-class benefits. Their staff enjoy such facilities as swimming pools, golf courses and picnic areas.

Some of the organizations make a special effort to bring workers and management together. They encourage everyone to feel that they are part of a team. Therefore, in these firms, all employees eat in the same canteen. Shopfloor workers do not wear blue overalls, but white shirts. Often, they are separated from office staff by only a glass partition.

The question is: if other firms provide similar pay and working conditions, will American business need unions in the future?

A Comprehension

1. Why are union leaders in the United States worried?

2. What change affecting the unions has taken place in the south?

3. How does a right-to-work law benefit a worker? Do you think it is a good law?

4. What does the example of the textile factory (para. 5) show?

5. Some northern firms prefer their shopfloor workers to wear white shirts. Why?

6. Why might American workers no longer need unions? Do you think such a situation is likely to arise? Explain your answer.

7. Explain the meaning of these words and phrases:

    elections (l. 5)
    a rural society (l. 8)
    do without them (l. 14)
    personnel policies (l. 22)
    shopfloor workers (l. 30)

B Vocabulary

1. Use the words in italics to complete the sentences. (You may have to use the *plural* form in some cases.)

benefit   *facility*   *management*   *membership*   *pay*
personnel   *trend*   *forbid*   *recruit*   *represent*

a) A lot of firms provide sports *facilities* for their employees.

b) In many factories, the management *forbids* workers to smoke on the shopfloor.

c) A *personnel* department selects staff and deals with employees' problems.

d) It is a duty of a union to *represent* its members.

e) A common type of *benefit* is a profit-sharing scheme.

f) Some southern companies do not want unions to *recruit* members inside their factories.

g) In some companies, worker representatives take part in *management* meetings.

h) Unions usually try to get *pay* increases for their members.

i) Since 1979, the *membership* of the United Automobile Workers' Union has been falling.

j) More and more companies are building canteens where managers and shopfloor workers eat together. This *trend* is likely to continue.

2. First, read the article. Then, find words or phrases in it which match the meanings given below.

NO END TO TRAIN DRIVERS' DISPUTE

by Peter Black
Industrial Correspondent

Train drivers will go on strike from next Monday unless the management agrees to accept their claim for a 5% pay increase. The drivers are also demanding a bonus for increased productivity.

Last night, the leaders of the URWU (United Railway Workers' Union) met the railways' management. Although they negotiated for over five hours, they were unable to reach agreement. The management asked the union to compromise and accept a pay rise of 3% but their offer was rejected.

Many people believe the two sides will not settle their dispute by bargaining. The Minister of Labour has said publicly: 'The only solution is an independent enquiry. The union and management representatives must go to arbitration.'

Meaning	Word/phrase
stop work	*GO ON STRIKE*
request for more money	CLAIM
special payment	BONUS

come to the same opinion ...AGREEMENT...

give way to some extent/accept less pay
than they were offered COMPROMISE

refused, turned down REJECTED

end an argument SETTLE a dispute

investigation/examination of a matter AN INDEPENDENT ENQUIRY

asking another person or group to
decide a matter ...ARBITRATION...

C Language Practice

First conditional
Train drivers *will go on* strike from next Monday, *unless* the management agrees
to accept their claim for a 5% pay increase.

If other firms *provide* similar pay and working conditions, *will* American
business need unions in the future?
Notice that the verb in the 'if' or 'unless' clause is in the present. The verb in
the clause of result is in the future.

Read the following:

The workers at a company have been on strike for several weeks. The company
director believes that if the strike continues, there will be serious problems for
the company, and that one problem will lead to another. These are the notes he
took with him to a meeting of the board.

Possible results of a continuation of the strike
Cancellation of two important overseas orders.
Fewer overseas orders because our customers will lose confidence.
Reduction in production.
Permanent shut-down of part of the plant.
No money for investment in new machinery.
Inability to compete with up-to-date companies.
Permanent closure of the whole factory.

Exercise 1

At the board meeting the director said: 'If two important overseas orders are
cancelled we'll get fewer overseas orders because our customers will lose
confidence.' Make similar comments, using the director's notes.

Exercise 2

Here are the workers' demands:
A 5% pay increase for all the workforce.
3 weeks' paid holiday.
A 35-hour working week.
Night work only once a fortnight.
Double pay for work on Sundays.
No work period to be longer than eight hours.

Example:

At the strike meeting the union leader said: 'We won't return to work unless we get a 5% increase in pay.'

Complete these outlines:

a) *We/stay out/strike/unless/get/three* . . .

b) *We/refuse/work/unless/management/offer/us/a 35-hour* . . .

c) *We/remain/strike/unless/we/only/work/night/* . . .

d) *The strike/continue/unless/management/pay/double* . . .

e) *There/be/no return/work/unless/no work period/be/longer* . . .

D Oral Work

Preparation   Persuading and convincing

Dick and Betty work in a factory which manufactures hi-fi equipment. They are both union representatives. Here, they are talking to the production manager, Jack Blunt, about a new rule that management has just introduced. Read or listen to the dialogue.

Betty: Look, Jack, we've been allowed to smoke here for years. You can't suddenly tell us to put out our cigarettes. Surely, you can see that.

Jack: I'm sorry, Betty, but that's the way it is. The smoking ban is management policy. It was decided at board level, you know.

Dick: Maybe, but don't you think someone should have talked to us first? No one said anything about a no-smoking rule at our monthly meetings.

Jack: Mmm . . . . I suppose it has come as a bit of a shock for you all.

Dick: That's right. The shopfloor workers don't like it when you people make new rules. We've got enough already.

Betty: Let's face it, Jack, this rule is going to cause a lot of trouble. We all enjoy a cigarette from time to time. It's our only pleasure.

Jack: Well, you'll have to give it up, I'm afraid.

Dick: Couldn't you ask the Board to think again? Everyone's very unhappy here at the moment. Look at the overtime we've been losing because of production problems.

Jack: Come on now, Dick. It's not our fault, is it? What's the use of producing goods if we aren't getting orders for them?

Betty: Listen, Jack. The point is that it's the wrong time to introduce the no-smoking rule.

Dick: Why don't you have a word with management? Tell them how we feel. Believe me, if you go through with the ban, you'll have a strike on your hands.

Jack: It's not as bad as that, surely? I tell you what I'll do. I'll think it over and come back to you on it later.

Practise these expressions

To persuade and convince:

Examples:

Surely you agree that workers need unions.
But don't you think the ban on smoking is necessary?
Let's face it, our working conditions have improved because of union action.

Two workers talk together in the canteen. One is a union representative.
He/she is convinced that employees need to be in a union. The other worker
does not believe in unions at all, so he/she has refused to become a union
member. Using the expressions listed below, note down some of the comments
that each worker makes to persuade the other to change his/her opinion.

But don't you think . . .
Believe me . . .
The point is that . . .
Surely . . .
Let's face it . . .
Look, . . .
Oh, come on now, . . .
Listen, . . .

Problem

Bill Hopkins is general manager of the factory where Jack Blunt works. Until
recently, there have been no serious labour problems, and relations between
management and workforce have been good.

Jack is now in Hopkins' office. For over an hour, he has been trying to make
the general manager change his mind about the no-smoking rule but Hopkins
just sits there shaking his head.

He thinks the rule is a good idea. In future, the shopfloor workers will have
to be more productive and improve the quality of their products. The reasons
for this are simple. Foreign manufacturers are competing strongly for a bigger
share of the hi-fi market. Also, in the past six months, customers have been
complaining that their sets have been breaking down. The new rule should
make the workers pay more attention to their work, so they will become more
efficient.

There is another point to remember. Next month, the firm is bringing out a
new stereo model. At that time, the production line must be working perfectly.

Of course, Hopkins knows the workers are unhappy. Last year, the company
laid off 10% of the workforce. This year, production has been falling because
shops have been placing fewer orders. Many workers have been losing overtime
pay, some have even been working short-time. It is true that the no-smoking
rule was announced rather suddenly, but perhaps this was the best way to
introduce an unpopular policy.

What do you think?

Divide into two groups, *management* and *union representatives*. The union members try to persuade the managers to change their no-smoking policy. One of you, playing the role of Bill Hopkins, leads the discussion.

Additional Discussion Topics

1. Some companies have a closed-shop policy—they *only* employ workers who are members of a union. Do you think companies should be allowed to have such a policy?

2. Some people believe that certain workers, for example those in hospitals, the police force, the electricity industry, etc., should not be permitted to go on strike. What do you think?

E Writing Exercise

After talking to the union representatives, Bill Hopkins attends a meeting of the board of directors. They decide *not* to change the no-smoking rule. Bill must now write to the representatives informing them of the decision and giving reasons for it.

  Imagine that you are Bill. Complete the memorandum which he has started writing. When you have finished it, sign it with your *initials* only. (A full signature is not necessary for memoranda.)

```
                         MEMORANDUM


    FROM:  General manager      DATE: 21 November, 19--

    TO:    Trade union
           representatives

    SUBJECT:  No smoking rule



    Thank you for meeting me on 14 November.  I am sure
    you all agree that we had a frank and useful discussion
    about the no smoking policy.

    On 19 November, I attended a board of directors
    meeting.  We talked for a long time ...
```

F Listening Comprehension

First, listen to the dialogue. Then, listen again, noting down information about Tom Bell in the appropriate spaces.

Name	TOM BELL
Age	. . . . . .
Work experience	. . . . . .
Reason for changing jobs	. . . . . .
Present salary	. . . . . .
Other benefits	. . . . . .
Working conditions before 1960	. . . . . .
Present working conditions	. . . . . .
Number of years employed by the company	. . . . . .
When does he retire?	. . . . . .

8 SKIS ROSSIGNOL

If you want to sell goods overseas, you can either export directly from your own country or you can set up a factory in the foreign market. What are the advantages and disadvantages of each method?

Skiing is a popular sport, enjoyed by people of all ages. The top skiers—the professionals—have usually been Europeans. It is the Austrians, French, Swiss and Italians who have produced the fastest times on the slopes. Recently, however, skiers from other countries have done well in international competitions. As a
5 result, interest in the sport has become worldwide.

A few years ago, the market for ski equipment was dominated by Austrian manufacturers. But then, a French company took over. Skis Rossignol is now the leading producer, with 25% of world ski sales.

The Rossignol group makes not only skis but also tennis rackets. It has an annual turnover of $150 million. Over 80% of its revenue comes from foreign sales, and 50% of those are from the United States. The domestic French market provides only 20% of its sales revenue.

The increasing popularity of skiing is one reason why the group has grown rapidly. Another reason is its multinational approach. Most ski manufacturers have based their factories in their home markets. Skis Rossignol has a different policy. It has set up production facilities close to its main foreign markets.

The managing director of the group is Mr Laurent Boix Vives. He explains why they had to do this. 'Skis have an international, not a domestic market. So, to increase our market share, we had to develop an international strategy.'

It took some years for the company to make that decision. When Boix Vives became managing director in 1958, his first task was to build up sales in France. He had to persuade people to buy Rossignol skis rather than imported ones. By skilful promotion, and increasing Rossignol's production capacity, he succeeded in doing this. The firm now has 50% of the French market.

In order to expand, Skis Rossignol had to break into the big foreign markets, such as the United States, Canada, Japan and Switzerland. First, the company tried increasing its exports to those countries. They set up marketing organizations and improved their distributor networks. However, by 1965 Boix Vives had decided that Rossignol would have to manufacture overseas.

There was one obvious disadvantage of manufacturing only in France. Because Rossignol exported most of its production, changes in exchange rates could greatly affect sales. If the franc rose sharply against the dollar or the yen, Rossignol's skis would become expensive in the United States and Japan.

In addition, there was a strong argument in favour of moving abroad. Boix Vives felt that the company had to stay close to its customers. As he says, 'We can't learn about foreign markets if we manufacture only in France'. Rossignol had to have first-hand knowledge of local conditions. In the United States, for example, skiing trends change fast. Skiers may suddenly wish to use short skis. As it now had a subsidiary in the States, Rossignol could quickly spot such a change and take advantage of it.

A Comprehension

1. What reason is given for the increased popularity of skiing worldwide?

2. What is the Rossignol group's turnover in France? (Give your answer in dollars.)

3. How did Mr Boix Vives build up sales in the French market?

4. What kind of international strategy did Skis Rossignol develop?

5. Why was the company worried about changes in exchange rates?

6. Explain the meaning of these words or phrases:

> *dominated* (l. 6)
> *took over* (l. 7)
> *skilful promotion* (l. 23)
> *production capacity* (l. 23)
> *distributor networks* (l. 28)
> *rose sharply* (l. 32)
> *first-hand knowledge of local conditions* (l. 37)
> *quickly spot such a change* (l. 39)

7. Why does Skis Rossignol prefer to have its own factory in the United States?

B Vocabulary

1. Complete these sentences, using the words in italics.

capacity	*network*	*task*	*revenue*
strategy	*subsidiary*	*trend*	*distributor*

a) Rossignol earns most of its . . . . . . from overseas markets.

b) The most important . . . . . . of a marketing director is to increase his firm's sales.

c) Usually, a company has to work out a different sales . . . . . . for each foreign market.

d) Setting up a . . . . . . in a foreign country is more expensive than using an agent.

e) If demand is weak, a factory may have to produce below . . . .

f) It takes time to build up a sales . . . . . . which will cover a whole country.

g) Manufacturers of fashionable clothes must be able to spot new . . . . . .s.

h) A big car manufacturer will probably have a number of . . . . . .s who have the right to sell its cars in certain areas.

2. Look at these verbs:

took over (l. 7)
set up (l. 16)
build up (l. 21)
break into (l. 25)

Such verb forms (verb + preposition or adverb) are common in English. Their meaning is often difficult to guess. You must just learn each form! Here are some useful expressions. Study them, then do the exercises.

Verb	*Meaning*
take over	to accept duties/responsibilities
take on	to start, to employ (a worker); to accept work, responsibility
take up	to begin a hobby, study, sport; accept an offer
take in	to trick, cheat someone
set up	to start, establish (a business, factory, etc.)
set out to	to begin a course of action
build up	to increase, develop
break into	to enter, penetrate (a market); to interrupt (a conversation)
break down	to stop working properly because of a fault or weakness; to divide and classify (figures), to explain in detail (expenditure)
break off	to end (talks, negotiations)
break up	to end (meeting)
break through	to make an important discovery (often used as a noun in the expression 'to make a breakthrough')

a) Complete these sentences.

(i) I shall take . . . . . . golf next winter.

(ii) We have taken . . . . . . 20 new workers.

(iii) People are often taken . . . . . . by fast-talking salesmen.

(iv) When Mr Boix Vives took . . . . . . as managing director of Skis Rossignol, he set . . . . . . to improve the company's sales in France.

(v) Breaking . . . . . . a new foreign market needs careful planning.

(vi) The meeting broke . . . . . . at 10 p.m.

(vii) You say our total publicity budget is £50,000. Could you break . . . . . . that figure please?

(viii) Our research department has made a break . . . . . . by designing a new type of ski.

b) Answer these questions. If possible, use the verbal phrases in italics in your answer.

(i) For what reasons do machines *break down*?

(ii) What should you find out before you *take up* the offer of a new job?

(iii) Which is the best area in your country to *set up* a factory? Explain your answer.

(iv)   What job would you like to *take on* if you were offered it?

(v)   If your boss asks you to *take on* extra work—without more pay—should you agree to do the work?

(vi)   What important breakthroughs have there been in the field of business?

C Language Practice

Second conditional

If the franc rose sharply against the dollar or the yen, Rossignol's skis *would become* expensive in the United States and Japan.

This is a statement about an imaginary situation which does not exist at the moment but which could happen. Here the second conditional is formed by using the past simple tense in the 'if' clause and *would* + the present participle in the clause of result.

McCready, a UK manufacturer of golf clubs and other golf equipment, found out the following facts about the American and Japanese markets.

	USA	Japan
Favourite style of golf clubs	American	American
Usual way of buying clubs	From golf teachers	From department stores and sports shops
Trade fairs	11	5
Number of regular players	25 million	8½ million
Number of golf courses	6,000	750

Exercise 1

Use the outlines below to complete the comments made by a UK golf equipment manufacturer who is considering whether to export to the USA and Japan.

Example:

If/we/sell/the USA/have to/sell/ . . . style clubs.
If we sold to the USA, we would have to sell American style clubs.

a) *If/we/enter/Japanese market/we/sell/department stores.*

b) *If/we/break into/US market/it/be/by contacting . . .*

c) *If/we/sell/Japan/our representative/attend/ . . . trade fairs.*

d) *If/we/market/USA/there/be/ . . . potential customers.*

e) *If/we/have/sales campaign/Japan/we/send/catalogues/to . . . golf course managers.*

What other comments can you make?

Exercise 2

Here is an extract from a report on Japanese golf club agents:

> . . . Japanese agents usually buy the stock from the manufacturer.
> However, they expect 50% of the cost of advertising to be paid for by
> the manufacturer. UK manufacturers do not find it worth exporting
> golf club bags and golfing clothes. They offer the agent a licence to
> manufacture these, using the UK label. Japanese agents expect regular
> visits from the UK manufacturer . . .

Managing director: What would the situation be if we exported to Japan?

Sales manager: Our agents would buy stock from us.

Use the extract from the report to make other possible answers to the
managing director's question.

D Oral Work

Preparation   Likes and preferences

*Courtex is an American tennis equipment manufacturer. From time to time, the
company sends staff to work in its overseas subsidiaries. Here, the head of overseas
marketing is talking to an executive who will go abroad for the firm next year.
Read or listen to the dialogue.*

Head/overseas marketing: I'm pleased you're going abroad for a while, Tracy. If you want to get on in this company, you have to spend some time in one of our overseas subsidiaries.

Tracy: Yes. That's the main reason I asked for the posting, actually.

Head/overseas marketing: Good. Now, is there anywhere you'd particularly like to go? You've probably thought about it a little.

Tracy: Yes, I'd prefer to go to Toronto if possible.

Head/overseas marketing: Any special reason?

Tracy: I was thinking . . . our company in Toronto is the biggest subsidiary. If I went there, I'd get plenty of experience. And probably have a responsible job.

Head/overseas marketing: Mmm, I'm not sure about Toronto. We've got a couple of executives there already. Is there anywhere else that interests you?

Tracy: I'd very much like to go to France—to our Paris subsidiary. I speak French fluently, so I could be useful there.

Head/overseas marketing: That's going to be difficult too. Someone else is keen to work in Paris—one of our senior executives.

Tracy: I see.

Head/overseas marketing:	How about Australia? We supply our Far Eastern markets from Sydney. That would be a good posting.
Tracy:	I'd rather not go there, really. Australia's so far away somehow.
Head/overseas marketing:	I see.
Tracy:	There is one other posting that attracts me. That's Athens.
Head/overseas marketing:	Ah, it doesn't surprise me. I'd love to work there as well. I've been to Greece many times. During my vacation, of course. It's a fascinating country.

Practise these expressions

To express likes and preferences:

Examples:

I'd very much like to change departments.
She's keen to spend some time overseas.
We'd prefer to use an agent in France rather than set up a subsidiary.

You are an executive in Courtex, and have been offered a period of training in one of these departments: sales; publicity; production; personnel; finance. Make comments about those choices, using the expressions given below.

1. I'd love to . . . .
2. I'd prefer . . . . . . than . . . .
3. I'd rather not . . . .
4. I'd also quite enjoy . . . . . . because . . . .
5. I'm very interested in . . . . . . , so . . . .
6. What really attracts me about . . . .

Problem

Courtex manufactures tennis equipment. It is based in Boston, USA, and has manufacturing subsidiaries and sales offices in several overseas areas. The company has a policy of sending executives abroad for one year as part of their training.

The executives are selected by a management team consisting of: the managing director, the head of overseas marketing, and the manager of staff development. At present, the team wishes to send executives to these areas: Toronto (Canada), Hong Kong (Far East), Riyadh (Saudi Arabia), Stockholm (Sweden), Hawaii (Pacific Ocean) and Paris (France).

The team has chosen six executives. It must now find out where each one wants to go. The managing director calls a meeting to hear each person's preferences. This kind of discussion is usually friendly—but frank!

What do you think?

You are either a member of the management team or one of the executives. Read the notes for your role before starting the meeting.

The leader of the discussion is the managing director. The management team must ask the executives where they want to go, and try to discover the reasons for their preferences. Then, both sides must work out a solution to the problem, even if some executives are not able to go to the country they first selected. (Only one posting in each country is allowed.)

Notes:

Management team
You already have some preferences of your own. If possible, you would like to send . . .

Alex to *Toronto:*   He is the most capable manager of the group. In three or four years' time, he could be managing director. Canada is your biggest overseas market.

Catherine to *Hong Kong:*   She has a university degree in oriental languages.

Pamela to *Hawaii:*   She is young and inexperienced. You do not want to give her too much responsibility. Hawaii is your smallest market.

James to *Saudi Arabia:*   The market is small but expanding fast. It has great potential. Your subsidiary there needs a hard-working executive who is able to get on well with people. James possesses these qualities.

Beatrice to *Paris:*   She speaks French fluently, and has travelled a lot in Europe. Your Paris subsidiary supplies the whole European market.

Larry to *Stockholm:*   He is young and dynamic. He will get on well with young Swedish tennis players. You hope he will persuade some of them to endorse your products.

Roles:

Executives

ALEX (age 40) Production manager
You would like to go to Hawaii. You have worked hard at the plant in Boston for over 20 years and now you need a rest. The subsidiary in Hawaii is a small one, so your job there would not be too difficult. If you can't go to Hawaii, you would like to spend a year in Saudi Arabia.

PAMELA (age 28) Assistant sales manager
You would prefer to go to Toronto because there is a big subsidiary there. It would offer you the opportunity to gain valuable experience. You are ambitious. You know that staff posted to Canada often receive quick promotion when they return to Boston. You do not want a posting to any other country.

JAMES (age 40) Salesman/technical adviser
Paris is your first choice for an overseas posting. The French subsidiary is

important because, at present, it supplies all the European markets. The experience of working there could be useful to you. Soon, Courtex is setting up sales offices in some European countries. You might be offered the position of sales manager in one of the offices.

CATHERINE (age 26) Publicity executive
You want to go to Saudi Arabia. You believe that this small but growing market could be important for the company in the future. If you work there for a year, you will have the chance to show your true abilities. At Boston, you work in a large department where promotion is slow.

BEATRICE (age 36) Design executive
There are only two postings you are interested in—Paris and Hong Kong. Both areas are centres of fashion. It would be exciting to work in either one because you would come in contact with other designers of tennis clothing. They would give you new ideas for creating fashionable garments.

LARRY (age 22) Assistant/contracts department
You are very keen to go to Saudi Arabia because staff who are posted there receive an excellent salary. They usually manage to save at least half of it, so they return to Boston with a useful sum of money to put in their bank. You need to save as much money as possible because you plan to marry after your posting.

Additional Discussion Topics

1. A friend of yours wants to set up a business in your country. He/she would like to manufacture an item of sports equipment. Which product would you advise your friend to choose? What should he/she do to build up its sales?

2. Which country would you like to go to for a one-year training period in a company? Why do you choose that country?

E Writing Exercise

At present, Courtex Inc. manufactures only tennis equipment. However, the marketing director would like them to make other sports goods and to enter new markets. In order to get ideas for new products, he is asking staff for their suggestions.

You are on a short training course at Courtex. One day, the marketing director asks you to write a short report on a sport which is becoming popular in your country. In the report, he hopes to find the answers to these questions:

Which sport is becoming popular?
Who plays it?
What kind of equipment and clothing do players use?
Where do people buy their equipment? Which manufacturers supply it?
What prices do people pay for it?
Should Courtex consider manufacturing the equipment? If so, how should it enter the market? By exporting directly from the USA? By using an overseas agent or salesman? Or by setting up a subsidiary?

F Listening Comprehension

1. First, listen to Janet reporting on her sales trip. As you do this, complete the data sheet, writing *notes* only.

DATA SHEET	*Area:* Far East
Product	
Market	
Popularity of tennis	
Methods of entering the market	1.
	2.
	3.
	4.
	5.

2. Listen to the report again. Then, working in *small groups*, provide answers to these questions:

   a) What does Janet Goodman say about each method of distributing their goods?

   b) Why won't Courtex set up a subsidiary in this overseas market?

   Compare your answers with those of the other groups.

9 FRANCHISING

Suppose you have a friend who wants to run his/her own business. He/she has little experience or capital (perhaps £10,000–£15,000). What advice would you give your friend?

Franchising is a means of marketing and distributing goods. The franchisor, normally a large business, supplies the franchisee, usually an individual, with products or services for sale to the public. The franchisee pays for the right to sell the product or service in a certain area, and also makes annual payments—known
5 as royalties—to the franchising company.

This type of business has always been popular in the United States. It developed particularly in the 1950s and 1960s when there was a boom in fast-food restaurants such as McDonald's and Kentucky Fried Chicken. Now about one-third of all retail sales in the US are through franchised outlets, and there are about 500,000
10 enterprises operating in this manner.

The system is spreading quickly throughout the world. In Europe companies using franchising include: Wimpy International (fast-food); Dayvilles (ice cream); Budget Rent-a-Car (car hire); Pronuptia (wedding dresses); Ziebart (car rust-proofing). Other countries are beginning to follow Europe's example. China is
15 producing and bottling Coca-Cola under a franchise agreement with the American company.

It is not surprising that franchising is growing fast. If it works properly, it has advantages for both sides. The franchisor is able to expand his business without reducing his capital or borrowing money. In fact he gets additional capital from an
20 outside source—the franchisee. Another advantage is that the franchise holders will probably be hard-working. This is important, especially in fast-food outlets where the hours of opening are long.

The franchisee gains from the arrangement as well. Franchisees are usually interested in business, but do not have much experience or capital. They want to
25 work for themselves, but are afraid to take too many risks.

To purchase a franchise, they may have to pay £20,000 or £30,000—part of which they can borrow from a friendly bank.

For their investment, franchisees buy the right to use the trade name of the franchisor, and they get advice about running the business. Also the franchising
30 company will provide them with training, materials and equipment. They will be able to take advantage of the company's specialized knowledge and its ability to buy in bulk. Finally, the franchisor will very likely be promoting the brand name of the business with national advertising.

The franchising system gives people the chance to set up in business without
35 taking great risks. If they choose their franchise wisely, they will have the opportunity to make a small fortune.

A Comprehension

1. Explain the meaning of these words or phrases:

   (i) *franchisor* (l. 1),   (ii) *franchisee* (l. 2),   (iii) *fast-food outlet* (l. 21),
   (iv) *brand name* (l. 32),   (v) *buy in bulk* (l. 32)

2. What facts show that franchising is becoming popular?

3. Why do companies use franchising to expand their business?

4. Why do people buy franchises?

5. What are the problems, do you think, of (a) being a franchising company, (b) running a franchise?

B Vocabulary

1. Complete the sentences using the words in italics. (Make any changes necessary.)

   investment outlet franchise capital retail royalty promote purchase boom distribute

   a) Franchised businesses are very common in the retail. trade.

   b) Many fast-food outlets. are run as franchises.

   c) You must pay a lot of money to buy the franchise. of a big hotel.

   d) The annual royalty. which a franchisee pays is usually a percentage of profits or turnover.

e) Many companies decide to *distribute* . . . . . . their goods by offering franchises to investors.

f) It is wise to get advice before you *purchase* . . . . a business.

g) Franchises appeal mostly to people who have limited *capital* . . . . . . to invest in a business.

h) In recent years, fast-food businesses have become popular in Britain. No one knows how long the . *boom* . . . will continue.

i) A franchise can be a good *investment* . . . . . for a person with little business experience.

j) Franchising companies generally spend a lot of money *promote* . . . . . . their goods.

2. Read this advertisement. Then, working in pairs, discuss the meanings of the words and phrases in the list which follows the advertisement. Compare your answers with those of other members of your group.

DO YOU WANT TO BE YOUR OWN BOSS?

The Chicken Pie boom has arrived!
50% gross expected this year.

We are an established company in the fast-food industry. We have over 40 outlets on carefully chosen sites. By running one of our franchised businesses, you can expect to earn gross profits in excess of £30,000 on a turnover of £60,000–£80,000 per annum. We provide:

★ training
★ equipment
★ high-quality food products
★ advice on shop lay-out
★ national advertising back-up

If you are the sort of person who enjoys a challenge, and who seeks the independence which comes from working for yourself, then this could be the opportunity you're looking for.

You must be willing to invest a minimum of £15,000. In return, we'll offer you a five-year contract with the option to renew on the same terms.

(*Note:* This offer would suit redundant executives or ex-army personnel who have a lump sum to invest.)

Call or write for more information to:
The Marketing Manager

---

a) *to be your own boss*
b) *established company*
c) *carefully chosen sites*
d) *gross profits*
e) *turnover*
f) *shop lay-out*
g) *back-up*
h) *a challenge*
i) *in return*
j) *option to renew*
k) *redundant executives*
l) *lump sum*

71

C Language Practice

May; can

The franchisee *may have to pay* twenty or thirty thousand pounds—part of which he *can borrow* from a bank.

The franchisee *may have to pay*. This means: Perhaps he will have to pay.

He *can borrow*. This means: It will be possible to borrow.

Rossarti's Ice Cream Franchise—Sales per Outlet

Study the bar chart and complete the exercises.
A member of Rossarti's sales staff is persuading someone to become a Rossarti Ice Cream franchisee.

1982 UK SALES PER OUTLET.
GALLONS PER WEEK

Exercise 1 (Work in pairs)
Example:

Franchisee: How much chocolate ice cream can I sell each week?

Salesman: Most weeks you can sell 16 gallons.

Franchisee: And in a good week?

Salesman: You may sell as many as 19 gallons.

Ask and answer questions about the other flavours of ice cream.

Exercise 2
Example:

'Usually a franchisee can sell 16 gallons of chocolate ice cream, but he may only sell 13.'

Make similar comments about the other flavours.

Exercise 3

Gross profit to the franchisee per gallon:

Chocolate £4   Orange £5
Coffee £3   Raspberry £3
Lime £3   Strawberry £4
Mint £5   Vanilla £5

'Most weeks a franchisee can make £64 on chocolate ice cream.'
'Some weeks he may make as much as £76. But he may make as little as £52.'

Make similar comments about the other flavours.

D Oral Work

Preparation   Making polite requests/checking information

A young woman, Angela Hart, is interested in running her own business. Seeing an advertisement in a newspaper for a fruit juice franchise, she phones for information. Read or listen to the dialogue.

Hart: Hello. I saw your advertisement in the *Daily Star*. I believe you're selling fruit juice franchises.

Advertiser: That's correct.

Hart: Could you give me some details, please?

Advertiser: Sure. Perhaps I'd better tell you something about us first. My name's Sean Tuke and my partner's Jeff Collins. We're from the USA.

Hart: I'm sorry, could you repeat that, please? Did you say your name's Snook?

Advertiser: No, Tuke. T-U-K-E.

Hart: Ah, I've got it now, thanks. And you're both Americans.

Advertiser: Right. We're setting up a franchise operation here in the UK and we're looking for hard-working people willing to invest money in a business.

Hart: I see. Can you tell me about the franchise, please? What sort of fruit juices do you sell?

Advertiser: We're in the business of marketing papaya juice.

Hart: Papaya juice? What on earth's that?

Advertiser: The papaya is a large fruit. It's sort of yellowy green in colour, and it comes from tropical countries.

Hart: Mmm . . . and obviously you can make fruit juice from it.

Advertiser: Yes, it's delicious. We think you British people are gonna love it.

Hart: Oh, you haven't actually sold any of the stuff yet?

Advertiser: No. But in the States we've several franchised outlets, and they're all going like a bomb.

Practise these expressions

To make polite requests:

Examples:

Could you tell me how much the franchise costs?
Can you come over and have a talk with me, please?
Would you mind explaining that once again, please?

To check information:

Examples:

I'm sorry, could you repeat that, please?
What exactly is a papaya?
Do you mean that you will choose a site for me?
Are you saying that the franchise is a bargain?

Work in pairs. One of you is selling a hotel franchise. The other has seen your advertisement in a magazine and is telephoning for further details. Using the expressions listed below, role-play part of the conversation.

Could you . . . ?
Would you mind . . . ?
I'd also like to know . . .
I wonder if you could tell me . . .
I'm sorry, could you repeat . . .
What exactly is . . . ?
Do you mean . . . ?
I'm not sure I understand . . .

Problem

Back home in Florida, USA, the Papjuz franchises have been a success. There are now over 50 outlets selling the papaya drink. Most operators are earning a living, and some of them, on the best sites, are making large profits.

Sean Tuke and Jeff Collins know why the franchises are doing well in Florida. First, Americans like fresh juice, which is just what they get at a Papjuz shop or stall. Each outlet has a special machine which peels the fruit, squeezes it, and produces the juice. Customers enjoy watching the machine in action. Secondly, Tuke and Collins have promoted the drink very cleverly. Their advertising creates an image of sunshine, good health and freshness.

The two Americans hope that Papjuz will become popular in Britain. They know that they will make a lot of money if they can sell 200 franchises in the next year or two. This is the offer they will make to investors: the franchisee will pay £5000 plus an annual royalty of £3000. In return he or she will receive a machine, cooling equipment, promotional materials, servicing and repairs. Papjuz will also help to find sites for the shops and stalls.

Tomorrow is Saturday. In a London hotel, Tuke and Collins will meet the first group of people who answered their advertisement. Will the two Americans be able to persuade these people to invest money in their franchises?

What do you think?

In this meeting, Sean Tuke and Jeff Collins try to persuade a group of people that Papjuz franchises are a good investment. The investors ask questions about the business and check carefully the information they are given.

Instructions:

Work in two groups, *franchisors* (Tuke/Collins) and *investors*. Before starting the meeting, *read the notes for your group only*. When the discussion has ended, the investors must decide if they wish to buy a Papjuz franchise.

Notes:

Franchisors

The figures below refer to expected costs, sales and profits, of a Papjuz franchise in the United Kingdom. Use the figures for your discussion with the investors. Try to have answers ready for all the questions they may ask you.

		£
Estimated sales per week	3000 cups of papaya at a price of 80p per cup	2400
Estimated costs per week	Franchise fee + royalty	150
	Paper cups	60
	50 cases of fruit (£30 per case)	1,500
	Wages	100
	Rent	100
Total cost per week		1,910
Gross profit per week		£490

Investors

Be careful! You do not want to lose your money. So, make sure you get all the facts and figures about the franchises. Here are some suggested questions—think of other questions you can ask.

You may want to know . . .

What the costs, sales and profits will be?
The selling price of a cup of papaya?
If British people will like the drink (how can the franchisors be sure)?
If the franchisors are providing advertising back-up (if so, what kind of advertising)?
What kind of contract are they offering (2 years/5 years/10 years)?
Where will the outlets be (in main streets/in stores/in hotels, etc.)?

E Writing Exercise

To attract investors, franchising companies usually place advertisements in newspapers or trade magazines. See the example in Section B of this unit.

Write an advertisement offering *one* of these franchised businesses to the general public:

a) A papaya juice outlet.

b) A new type of fast-food franchise.

c) A car-care business (cleaning cars inside and outside and repairing seats and upholstery).

d) A fast-printing shop (serving shops, offices and other customers; using up-to-date, electronic machinery, e.g. colour copiers and word processors).

F Listening Comprehension

Listen to the dialogue. Then listen again, and answer these questions.

1. Where did Donna get her information about McDonald's restaurants?
   ARTICLE IN A MAGAZINE
2. What does Donna say when Pierre mentions 'hamburger and chips'?
   FRENCH FRIES
3. What do Wendy and Pierre think of the food in McDonald's restaurants?
   W → LOVES   P → PREFER FRENCH
4. Who is Mr Dayan?
   HE IS THE FRANCHISER
5. How many outlets does he run?
   14
6. Why are McDonald's unhappy with the Paris franchises? What do they want to do now? *FOOD BAD, BAD SERVICE   PLACES DIRTY*
7. In Mr Dayan's opinion, why are McDonald's saying bad things about his businesses? *MC WANTS CONTROL ABOUT HIS BUSINESS*
8. When did the franchising company sign a contract with Mr Dayan? What do we know about the contract? *A GOOD DEAL BY THAT TIME*
9. What happened in 1976? *BUSINESS STARTED BOOMING*
10. Why are the French fries better in the United States, according to Wendy?
    POTATOES

10 MALAYSIAN TAKEOVER

What is a takeover bid? Why do some bids succeed and others fail?

The Guthrie Corporation owns rubber, tea and cocoa plantations in Malaysia. Until 1981, it was British-based, being owned mainly by British shareholders. These were either big institutions, like investment trusts and insurance

Malayan rubber plantation workers.

companies, or small private investors. However, one morning in September,
ownership of Guthrie suddenly changed hands. In the space of four hours, a
Malaysian Government agency, Permodalan, bought control of the business.
People say it was the fastest takeover in the history of the London Stock Exchange.

This is what happened. The Malaysians already owned 25% of the corporation.
They used the London stockbrokers, Rowe and Pitman, to increase their stake in
it. They began the day by offering to buy 5% of the company's shares for 901
pence each. The market price was then 662 pence. The big investors jumped at the
chance to sell at such a favourable price. By lunchtime, Rowe and Pitman had
spent £72 million and obtained 25.5% of the plantation group's shares. At the
same time, Permodalan managed to buy a further 10% of the shares from
Malaysian shareholders. Since it now had a shareholding of well over 50%, it
controlled the Guthrie Corporation.

After making its successful bid, Permodalan offered to buy the remaining shares
in the company. A month later, Guthrie's directors recommended shareholders to
accept the offer, though they thought the price of 901 pence did not reflect the true
value of the business. They explained that only a small number of shares would
remain in independent hands, so the market for those shares would be limited.
Their price would probably fall below 901 pence.

Everyone in the financial world was surprised at the speed of the takeover.
Newspapers described it as a 'dawn raid' on the Stock Exchange. Most people
admired the way in which it had been planned and carried out. However, some
criticized the bid. One person said 'It is wrong that people can get control of a
business so quickly without informing the majority of the shareholders'.

Why did Permodalan take over Guthrie? First, the Malaysian Government
wanted to have control of important resources such as rubber and cocoa. Secondly,
it was worried that the corporation was moving further away from South-East
Asia. In recent years, Guthrie had diversified its business activities, buying
companies in other parts of the world. For example, it had just invested $68
million in the American company, Page Airways. Permodalan decided a takeover
was necessary to protect its already large investment in Guthrie.

A Comprehension

1. What was unusual about this takeover?

2. Why was the bid successful?

3. In what ways was the takeover a *skilful* action?

4. Explain the meaning of these words or phrases:
   investment trust (l. 3)
   stake (l. 9)
   independent hands (l. 21)
   dawn raid (l. 24)
   to protect its already large investment (l. 33)

5. Can you suggest reasons why Guthrie had been moving away from South-East Asia and diversifying its activities?

6. How did people feel after the takeover bid was announced?

B Vocabulary

1. Use the words in italics to complete the sentences. (Make any changes necessary.)

   activity bid control investment offer
   shareholding stake ownership

   a) The Malaysians already had a . . . . . . of 25% in Guthrie.

   b) The corporation was involved in many business . . . . . .s.

   c) You obtain . . . . . . of a company by acquiring more than 50% of its shares.

   d) Guthrie had a . . . . . . in many companies operating outside Malaysia.

   e) We made an . . . . . . of £6 per share, but it was not accepted by the shareholders.

   f) A takeover . . . . . . is likely to succeed if a high price is offered for a company's shares.

   g) There is a lot of foreign . . . . . . in Canada and France, but little in Japan.

   h) . . . . . . of oil and steel companies is often in the hands of governments.

2. Talking about graphs. Here are some phrases you can use to describe *points* or *changes* in a graph (the examples refer to share prices). Study the phrases, then do the exercise.

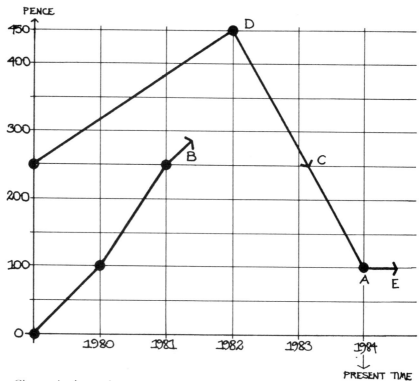

Changes in share prices.

79

Examples:

a) *To stand at*
   At present, the share price stands at 100 pence.

b) *To increase by/to; to rise by/to; to go up*
   An increase of; a rise
   In 1980, the share price increased by 150 pence/increased to 250 pence.

c) *To decrease by/to; to fall by/to; to go down*
   A decrease of; a fall
   In 1982, the share price went down by more than 150 pence/went down to about 280 pence.

d) *To reach a peak of*
   At the beginning of 1982, the share price reached a peak of 450 pence.

e) *To level off*
   In 1984, the share price is expected to level off.

Look at this graph showing changes in Guthrie's share price over a four-year period. (*Note:* Sime Darby is the name of another company which tried to take over Guthrie, but failed.)

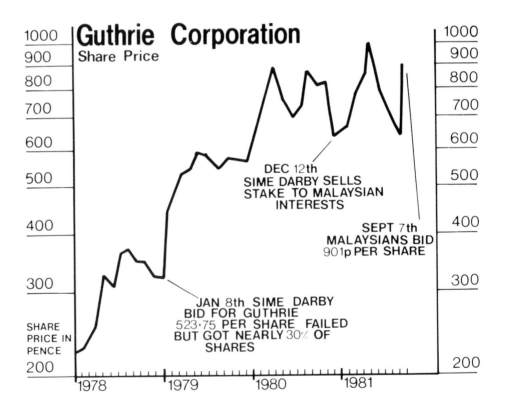

Guthrie Corporation
Share Price

DEC 12th
SIME DARBY SELLS
STAKE TO MALAYSIAN
INTERESTS

SEPT 7th
MALAYSIANS BID
901p PER SHARE

JAN 8th SIME DARBY
BID FOR GUTHRIE
523·75 PER SHARE FAILED
BUT GOT NEARLY 30% OF
SHARES

SHARE
PRICE IN
PENCE

1978   1979   1980   1981

Write five sentences describing the points and changes in the price of the share.

Example:

At the beginning of 1978, the share price stood at about 230 pence.

C Language Practice

After making its successful bid, Permodalan offered to buy the remaining shares.

Before taking over the company, Permodalan already owned 25% of the shares.
    When a verb immediately follows *before* or *after* it takes '-ing'.

Read the following and complete Exercise 1.

When Aldex International took over Mudon plc, they appointed their own team of senior personnel. This table shows the stages the selection panel went through to select a new production manager.

1. Advertised in the national press and specialist magazines.
2. Sent out recruiting letters to executives in other companies.
3. Sifted through the letters from applicants.
4. Rejected all unsuitable applicants.
5. Made a short-list of the eight most suitable applicants.
6. Invited the eight for interviews.
7. Held preliminary interviews.
8. Rejected five of the applicants.
9. Held in-depth interviews with the remaining applicants.
10. Selected the best person for the job.

Exercise 1
Join the items on the list as in the examples.

Examples:

After advertising in the national press and specialist magazines, they sent out recruiting letters to executives in other companies.

Before sending out recruiting letters to executives in other companies, they advertised in the national press and specialist magazines.

They began the day *by offering* to buy 5% of the company's shares. It is wrong that people get control of a business so quickly, *without informing* the majority of the shareholders.
    When a verb immediately follows a preposition it takes '-ing'.

Read the following and complete Exercise 2.

Here are some comments made in the press about the Aldex International takeover of Mudon plc:

'They have kept some of the senior staff because they have offered them excellent salaries.'

'When they made the takeover bid, they already had a large shareholding in the company.'

'Since they got control of the company, they have appointed their own senior executive team.'

'They appointed new heads of department, although they did not tell the rest of the staff.'

'Aldex International have gained favour with the government because they have started a new training scheme.'

'After Aldex International appointed the new management team, Aldex made a number of changes in Mudon's company structure.'

'Since Aldex made the changes in the company's structure, they have made it more efficient.'

Exercise 2

Rewrite the comments from the press as in the examples.

Examples: They have kept some of the senior staff *by offering* them excellent salaries.

When making their takeover bid, Aldex International already had a large shareholding in the company.

D Oral Work

Preparation   Making predictions: certainty, probability and possibility

This is a telephone conversation between the chairman of a company, Andrew Cowley, and its financial director, Lyn Ashton. The chairman discusses a takeover bid which a large organization is about to make for their business. Read or listen to the dialogue.

Andrew: Hello, Lyn, Andrew here.

Lyn: Hello, Andrew. How did things go this morning?

Andrew: Not too well, I'm afraid.

Lyn: Oh, I'm sorry to hear that. What happened exactly?

Andrew: Well, I had a long talk with Frank Bowman, their chief executive.

Lyn: Uh huh.

Andrew: He was absolutely frank with me. They're definitely going to make a bid. He's even told me the price they'll offer for our shares—180p.

Lyn: 180p? Do you reckon our shareholders will sell at that price?

Andrew: They might, but it's rather unlikely, I'd say.

Lyn: So what are we worrying about, then?

Andrew: Bowman thinks the shareholders will probably accept the offer if we advise them to.

Lyn: What? Recommend that they sell out to IIC at 180p a share? There's no chance of our doing that, surely.

Andrew: None at all. We're certainly going to oppose this bid, Lyn. We'll fight tooth and nail if we have to—I can promise you that.

Lyn: That's good to hear.

Andrew: I tell you one thing, Lyn, we could lose if we don't play our cards right.

Lyn: How do you mean?

Andrew: Oh, Bowman said one or two things that . . . er . . . worried me . . . . Look, Lyn, could we discuss this back at the office? I'll be there at about four.

Lyn: Four? Mmm, that might be a bit tricky. I'll be in a meeting at that time, but I should be free by about 4.30. Is that OK?

Andrew: Fine. See you later then.

Lyn: Right. Goodbye.

Practise these expressions

To express certainty:

Examples:

They're definitely going to make changes in the company.
We're certainly going to refuse their offer.
There's no doubt that we'll win.

To express probability:

Examples:

They'll probably make another bid for our company.
There's a good chance that they'll succeed this time.

To express possibility:

Examples:

The shareholders might sell their shares.
We could have a talk with their chairman.

To express improbability:

Examples:

It's unlikely that I'll be free at that time.
There's not much chance that they'll keep the present directors.

Using the expressions listed below, make predictions about your own future. Or, if you prefer, predict the futures of other members in your group!

Example:

There's a good chance that . . .
There's a good chance that I'll change my job soon.

There's no doubt that . . .
There's a good chance that . . .

I'm probably going to . . .
It's rather unlikely that . . .
I might . . .
. . . could . . .
. . . is definitely going to . . .
There's no chance of . . .

Problem

Andrew Cowley is chairman of Kondor plc, an engineering firm based in Birmingham, England. Kondor makes products for the car and aircraft industries, as well as military equipment for foreign governments. At present, it is negotiating with a Middle East country to supply components for a new weapons system. If it wins the contract, the company will have full order books for the next five years.

The American-based IIC group intends to take over Kondor. IIC has huge cash reserves, which it uses to snap up smaller companies. In recent years, it has acquired a number of firms in different areas of business. 'We have a finger in every pie,' Frank Bowman told Cowley at their meeting.

The voting shares of Kondor are distributed among shareholders as follows:

Shareholder	Shareholding	Notes
IIC	10%	The holding was acquired by IIC's stockbrokers a month ago at a price of 130 pence.
Investment agency	8%	The agency acts for a South American government.
Two insurance companies	7%	
Kondor's directors	2%	
Other shareholders	73%	These are all small private shareholders.

Kondor would be a good acquisition for IIC. Its present share price—140 pence—is low and does not reflect the true value of the company. Kondor's profit record during the last three years has been poor. Lost contracts, heavy expenditure on research to develop new products, and rising operating costs have been the cause of this.

IIC are not only attracted by the low share price. They also know that Kondor has valuable assets: an impressive office block in the centre of Birmingham; three modern factories; a large piece of land outside Birmingham, suitable for building on. All these assets were entered into the accounts years ago, and have not been revalued.

Cowley's meeting with Bowman had been friendly until he had mentioned that Kondor's board would probably advise shareholders to hold on to their shares.

'If you do that, we shall increase our offer to 220 pence a share. They'll certainly sell at that price,' Bowman had said. 'Possibly,' Cowley had replied.

'Of course they will,' said Bowman, 'but I warn you . . . if we have to pay too much to get control of Kondor, then we'll have to get our money back somehow. Perhaps by selling some of Kondor's assets or by reducing the workforce—not just factory workers, but managers and even directors!'

What do you think?

There are eight members of Kondor's board of directors. The board now meets to consider this question: should they advise the shareholders to accept IIC's offer of 180 pence a share when that offer is announced?

Instructions:

Each student plays one of the roles described below. The leader of the discussion is Kondor's chairman. (*Note:* To reach a decision, you may have to take a vote at the end of the meeting.)

Roles:

Chairman
You lead the discussion. Ask all the directors to give their opinions and encourage them to speak frankly. Personally, you want to advise the shareholders *not* to acept IIC's offer. If they are told the full facts about the company—the contract with the Middle East company, the undervalued assets, etc.—they will definitely hold on to their shares. You think the shares are worth at least 250 pence.

Joint managing director
In your opinion, the board should advise shareholders to accept the offer. If IIC pays only 180 pence for the shares, they will be pleased and will probably keep the present directors. You don't want to lose your job. Besides receiving a high salary, you live in a company-owned house and have the use of a chauffeur-driven car.

Joint managing director
The board should advise shareholders to accept the offer. You think Kondor needs IIC's financial backing. It is becoming more and more expensive to manufacture military equipment and develop new products. If IIC invests money in Kondor, the company will probably be more competitive, and should be able to spend more on marketing its products.

First director
You want to advise shareholders *not* to accept the offer. They will certainly hold on to their shares if the board gives them full information about the company's assets and future prospects. The directors should recommend that they refuse all offers below 250 pence a share.

Second director
Kondor should advise the shareholders to accept the offer. In your opinion, the company's future prospects are poor. They have no chance of winning the contract with the Middle East country (several other companies are competing for it). You have heard that the investment agency and the two insurance companies have privately agreed to sell their shareholding to IIC. Sooner or later, IIC will buy enough shares to get control of Kondor.

Third director

Kondor should advise the shareholders *not* to accept the offer. You think the shares are worth at least 280 pence. You are certain the shareholders will follow the chairman's advice. You are worried about IIC. Who *really* owns the group? Is there an unknown foreign government in the shadows?

Fourth director

You are not sure what advice to give. (Decide at the end of the meeting.) On the one hand, you think IIC could lose interest and go away if they don't buy enough shares at 180 pence. On the other hand, perhaps Kondor should be taken over. It certainly needs new managers, one or two more directors—and more cash.

Fifth director

You are not sure what advice to give. (Decide at the end of the meeting.) On the one hand, you do not like IIC's reputation. They often buy companies, then sell off their assets. Also, they are likely to get rid of workers if they take over Kondor. On the other hand, Kondor's profit record has been poor. New owners might make changes which would improve its performance.

Additional Discussion Topics

1. Should dawn raids on the Stock Exchange be allowed?

2. Is a person *gambling* when he buys shares on the Stock Exchange? Give reasons for your answer.

E Writing Exercise

The advertisement below will appear in several national newspapers. It will be signed by Kondor's chairman. Complete it by writing additional paragraphs. Advise the shareholders what to do about IIC's offer and explain why you are recommending that course of action.

KONDOR plc

Message to our shareholders

On 2 July, the American investment group, IIC, will make a formal offer to buy 40% of Kondor's shares at a price of 180 pence. Since IIC already have a 10% shareholding, and expect to acquire another 15% from other sources, the purpose of their bid is clearly to get control of our company.

We strongly advise shareholders . . . . . .

F Listening Comprehension

Listen to the tape twice. While you do so, take notes. Then complete these sentences with information from the tape.

1. As a result of the new rule, a company cannot . . . .

2. If a bidder wants to buy more than 5% of a company's shares, he must . . . .

3. The waiting time is also called a . . . .

4. There are three advantages of the waiting period.
   First, ...
   Second, ...
   Third, ...

5. Some 'dawn raids' have been so fast that . . . .

6. Mr Robert James wanted to acquire . . . .

7. Mr James was delighted . . . .
   He thinks the shares are . . . .
   However, the interviewer pointed out that the amount of shares he bought was well below . . . .

8. Mr James was unable to buy enough shares because . . . .

9. At the end of the day, the shares . . . .

10. The Chairman of London Printing House was not too disappointed because . . . .

11 SMALL WEDDING IN CHINA

What is a joint venture? Why do firms make such arrangements? Can you give an example of a joint venture?

Veronica Moss is a small British firm which makes wedding dresses. It is now expanding into European markets but, to be successful, it needs to increase its production and keep costs as low as possible. Recently the firm has not been able to depend on a regular production of dresses. Labour turnover has been high, and it
5 has been difficult to get workers to do overtime.

To solve the problem the managing director, Mr Gwillim, looked for other ways of making the wedding clothes. In the end he came up with an interesting solution. This was to have a joint production agreement with a Chinese corporation. Under the agreement, a factory in the province of Guandong (South China) will
10 manufacture dresses for the European market and share production costs with Veronica Moss.

It took Mr Gwillim less than a year to arrange the deal with the Chinese. This was unusually quick. Luckily, he was helped by a Chinese businessman now living in England but who originally came from Tungwan, in Guandong. This man, who
15 was experienced at dealing with Chinese trade officials, gave useful advice during the negotiations.

There was another reason why the deal was completed quickly. At present, China is encouraging foreign investment—especially in the south. The government knows that the country needs foreign help to modernize its industry.
20 Also joint ventures with overseas companies create employment and earn foreign currency. To make deals easier to arrange, the government is allowing provincial officials to negotiate directly with foreign businessmen.

Veronica Moss's contract is a fairly standard one for this type of venture. The Chinese will provide the factory, which is rent-free, and the workers. They will
25 produce 1000 garments a week, which the British firm will buy at a price of £1.50 each. In addition, a 5% annual price increase has been written into the contract for each of the next ten years.

Veronica Moss will invest £50,000 in the project. Half of this will be used to install machinery, such as cutting and stitching machines. The rest will be spent
30 on renovating the interior of the building. All the patterns, measurement specifications and cloth will be supplied by the British.

The management of the factory will be shared. While the manager and technical director have been appointed by the Chinese, the British firm has chosen a Chinese executive as advisor on quality control.

35   When the garments are finished, they will be delivered to customers in Europe and Scandinavia. Recently, Veronica Moss has been considering using Chinese-made fabrics such as silk to make wedding dresses. Although the dresses would be expensive, they might appeal to buyers in the United States—the biggest market for wedding clothes.

40   The 'wedding' between Veronica Moss and the Chinese corporation is special. It is the first joint production agreement to be negotiated directly between a British firm and a Chinese one. No embassy or government was directly involved in the deal.

A Comprehension

1. Why did Mr Gwillim arrange a joint venture with a Chinese firm?
2. In what way, if any, did the Chinese government help the British company?
3. What advantages does Veronica Moss get because of the contract?
4. How do the Chinese benefit from the joint venture?
5. Why do you think Veronica Moss chose an overseas executive to advise on quality control?
6. What do these words or phrases in the text mean?
   labour turnover (l. 4)
   came up with (l. 7)
   a fairly standard one (l. 23)
   has been written into the contract (l. 26)
   measurement specifications (l. 30)
7. What is unusual about this joint venture?

B Vocabulary

1. Complete the sentences, using the words in italics. (Make any changes necessary.)

   turnover   deal   venture   specification   pattern   negotiate   modernize install   renovate   appoint

   a) The Chinese do not decide on the length of the dresses. They work according to the British firm's . . . .
   b) . . . . . . contracts with Chinese corporations can often take more than a year.
   c) It can be a profitable business to . . . . . . old houses, then sell them.
   d) If staff . . . . . . in a company is high, the employees are probably dissatisfied with their working conditions.
   e) If you want to make a . . . . . . with the Chinese, you must be patient.
   f) When making a garment, a dressmaker usually works from a . . . .
   g) When your plant and equipment become out-of-date, it is time to . . . . . . your factory.
   h) When a company sets up a foreign subsidiary, it often . . . . . . local staff to management positions.
   i) Any . . . . . . involving cooperation with a foreign firm is likely to be risky.
   j) Workers are sometimes unhappy when their firm . . . . . . new machines. They are afraid of losing their jobs because of them.

2. Look at this example:

   He *came up with* an interesting solution (l. 7).

Here are some other verbs + prepositions/adverbs. They are used when talking of negotiations, deals and projects. Study them, then do the exercise.

> *break off* (negotiations)—stop, withdraw from
> *come across* (someone, something)—meet or find by chance
> *come up with* (idea)—think of
> *come up against* (difficulty)—meet, run into
> *cope with*—manage to deal with
> *carry out* (plan)—put into practice
> *draw up* (contract)—prepare and write
> *fall through* (plan, project)—fail (e.g. Our plan fell through)
> *set up* (deal)—arrange
> *put forward* (idea, suggestion)—present, suggest

Now, practise using the above verbal phrases by completing this text. A businessman is talking about a joint venture with a Chinese firm.

'We have a factory in Hong Kong which makes cassettes. One day, one of my managers came . . . . an interesting idea. He said, "Why don't we assemble some of our cassettes in China? It'll be much cheaper." However, we were not sure how to set . . . . . . this kind of deal, so we did nothing for a while. Then, one day, I came . . . . . . a Hong Kong businessman, called Mr Soong. He had good contacts in China and offered to help us carry . . . . . . our plan to manufacture there. He contacted a manufacturer in Guandong and set up a meeting with the management. We were able to put . . . . . . a number of proposals at that meeting. Everything went smoothly at first, but then we came . . . . . . against a difficulty. They wanted *us* to pay the local 30% corporation tax on profits. We couldn't agree, and soon we were on the verge of breaking . . . . . . negotiations with them. Then, I came up with a solution to the problem. We would each pay half of the tax! After that, we drew . . . . . . a contract and were ready to put the scheme into operation. Later on, we had to cope . . . . . . various problems—quality control was tricky—but everything's going well now. Thank goodness our project didn't fall . . . . . . because we didn't agree about tax!'

C Language Practice

Veronica Moss is a small British firm *which makes wedding dresses*. A Chinese businessman *who was from Guandong* helped him.

The italic sections are *defining clauses*, which identify *who* or *what* is being spoken about. No commas are used.

This Chinese businessman, *who was experienced*, gave useful advice. The Chinese provide the factory, *which is rent-free*.

The italic sections are *non-defining clauses*, which give extra information about something. Commas separate them from the main clause.

Read the following, then do the exercise.

In 1982 Wedding Bells, a small firm which makes wedding dresses, collected information about their best-selling dresses from their regional sales managers.

Sales manager	Style	Description	Retail price
Mr Krantz (London)	Belle	Cotton & Lace	£549*
	Cilla	Georgette & Lace	£689
Mrs Holly (North-east)	Nymph	Cotton & Voile	£478*
	Belle	Cotton & Lace	£549
Mrs Marks (North-west)	Gina	Nylon & Lace	£399*
	Cilla	Georgette & Lace	£689
Mr Bloom (South-west)	Nymph	Cotton & Voile	£478*
	Gina	Nylon and Lace	£399

* Best-sellers.

Exercise

Several wedding dress wholesalers met to discuss trade. Here are some of the comments overheard at their meeting.

'A man who works for Wedding Bells told me a cotton and lace dress was their best seller in London.'

'Mr Krantz, who works for Wedding Bells, told me Cilla was their second best-seller in London.'

'Cilla, which is made of georgette and lace, is Wedding Bells' second best-seller in London.'

'A dress which is made of cotton and lace is Wedding Bells' best-seller in London.'

Using Wedding Bells' table of regional best-sellers, make similar comments of your own.

D Oral Work

Preparation   Expressing regret about the past

Brian and Edward are executives in a company manufacturing toys. They are discussing one of their products—a model motor cycle. It has been made in Hong Kong under a joint venture agreement.

Brian: It's all my fault, Ed. I shouldn't have let the Hong Kong factory make the toy. Now, look what's happened.

Edward: It wasn't only you who made that decision, Brian. It was all of us. Anyway, the factory's done a good job. They've produced a superb product.

Brian: That's the trouble, isn't it? Everyone wants to buy the motor cycle, but we can't meet the demand for it. It's annoying—just when we had a winner at last.

Edward: Yes. Quite honestly, I wish we'd made the toy over here too. Still, it's no use crying over spilt milk.

Brian: I suppose not. It's just that I can't help feeling guilty. I should have kept in closer touch with the Hong Kong factory. If only I'd gone over there more often.

Edward: It wouldn't have made any difference, Brian. We've been unlucky, that's all. Things happen, unexpectedly . . .

Brian: The new machines, you mean?

Edward: Yes.

Brian: Look, Ed. It's quite simple. We should have realized that the machines wouldn't arrive on time. It was our fault—there's no doubt about that at all.

Practise these expressions

To express regret about the past:

Examples:

I shouldn't have signed that agreement.
I wish we had been more careful.
If only I had known the product would be so successful.

Imagine that you are the owner of a small toy firm which has just gone bankrupt. You are feeling sorry for yourself because you now believe the bankruptcy could have been avoided.

Using the expressions listed below, write sentences expressing regret about the past.

Example:

If only . . .
If only we hadn't tried to produce so many products.

> *I wish we had . . .*
> *I regret that we didn't . . .*
> *I should have . . .*
> *If only our competitors . . .*
> *I'm sorry our research department didn't . . .*
> *I wish our export manager . . .*
> *If only the retail shops . . .*
> *Our marketing department should have . . .*

Problem

Brian is a director of a British company, Wellington Toys plc. His friend, Edward, is the sales manager for the home market. Edward has only been in the job about 18 months. He enjoys it but does not find it easy. Managing a sales force of 30 (24 representatives and 6 area managers) requires a good deal of skill and energy. Until recently, though, he thought his department was in good shape.

Suddenly, a problem arose with a new product—a model motor cycle. This toy was made for Wellington by a Hong Kong manufacturer under a joint venture agreement. Normally, such an expensive and complicated model would be made in the British factory. However, the management—and especially Brian—insisted on producing it in Hong Kong because costs were lower there. 'If the toy is successful,' they said, 'we'll make a lot of money from it.'

Wellington needs money badly. Recently, it has been going through a difficult time. Foreign competition and a strong pound have caused profits to fall, both in home and overseas markets.

The model motor cycle was put on the market in January. At the trade fairs in February and March, it attracted everyone's attention. People admired the beautifully made model of an old but famous motor cycle. A trade journal named it 'Toy of the Year'. Immediately, Edward's sales team made every effort to persuade retailers that the toy was worth its price of £45.

The sales representatives had no difficulty in selling the model. Orders came in fast during March and April for delivery in June. It soon became clear that extra production capacity would be necessary in Hong Kong to meet demand. Ken Li, the Chinese manager, ordered new machine tools from his German supplier. But these failed to arrive in May, when they were needed for the increased production of the model cycle. Li telexed Brian and Edward, saying 'delivery will be delayed at least six weeks'.

It is now early July. The machine tools have still not arrived, and production of the new toy has been seriously held up. This is because of a long strike at the German supplier's factory. Ken Li has been unable to get the tools from another source.

Edward is in a difficult situation. His sales force are very unhappy. Two months ago, they were working night and day to get bulk orders; now they are telling customers to hang on just a little longer. Three representatives are already talking of resigning.

Worst of all, his top salesman, Peter Bristol, has booked a two-week holiday in Hawaii for himself and his wife. It's their 20th wedding anniversary. The holiday starts on 2 August. Pete expects to pay for it out of the commissions he will receive from orders for the toy. 'If I don't get the money in time, and have to put off my holiday, I'll leave Wellington,' he says. Like everybody else, Pete knows that commissions are based on *invoiced* orders. And invoices are only made out when the goods are ready for despatch.

What do you think?

The management team meets for an informal discussion, led by Brian and Edward. They consider these questions:

1. What mistakes have been made in this situation?

2. How serious is the problem? Does it show weaknesses in the firm and its management?

3. What actions should Peter take now?

4. What should the company do so that such a situation does not occur again?

Instructions:

You are all members of the management team. You should take the opportunity during the discussion to *express regrets* and to *criticize* each other.

Additional Discussion Topics

1. Four manufacturers, selling in world markets, want to set up co-production deals. Henry (England) has a high-class shoe business; Juan (Spain) has a firm which makes tractors; Birgitta (Sweden) owns a baby clothes company; Simone (France) has a furniture company.

   In which of these areas should each set up a joint production deal? (Give reasons for your choices.)
   (i) China   (ii) The Soviet Union   (iii) The United States
   (iv) Saudi Arabia   (v) Japan   (vi) A South American country.

2. In which country would *you* prefer to have a joint venture? Why?

E Writing Exercise

The following advertisement appears in the business section of a newspaper:

Joint venture opportunity

Hong Kong-based publishing company is interested in setting up joint production projects with western firms. Write, with brief details of your proposal, to: Mr Y. Soong, Happy Valley Publishing Co., Kowloon, H.K., Far East.

You are the managing director of a publishing company. Because production costs in your country are increasing fast, you are considering printing part of your book output abroad. Reply to Mr Soong's advertisement, giving details of: the size of your firm (annual turnover, gross profits, number of employees, etc.); the type of books you publish; the scope of your business (e.g. in which markets you sell, whether you use agents or subsidiaries to distribute your books abroad, etc.). Then, explain clearly the kind of joint production you are interested in. Finally, suggest that you meet him either in your country or Hong Kong.

F Listening Comprehension

Listen to the tape twice, noting down information about the photocopy agreement. Then complete this newspaper article which is based on it.

U.S. firm makes deal with Chinese

An agreement has just been signed between . . . . . . and the . . . . . . for the supply of . . . . . . and also components for another 5,000.

China will pay . . . . . . dollars for the machines and technology.

In addition, the US company will help the Chinese to manufacture at least . . . . . . a year in the future. These will be sold in both . . . . . . and . . . . . . markets.

Clark Copy International is a small company, ... in Chicago. It won the contract in the face of competition from . . . . Its chief executive believes his company was successful because . . . .

In the next five years, the American company are expected to earn

. . . .

It is likely that, thanks to this success, other Western firms will be encouraged to make deals with Chinese corporations. Clearly, business relations between China and the West will continue to improve.

---

12 *THE EEC TEXTILE INDUSTRY*

Which industries in your country are most affected by foreign competition? Should your government protect those industries against such competition? If so, how?

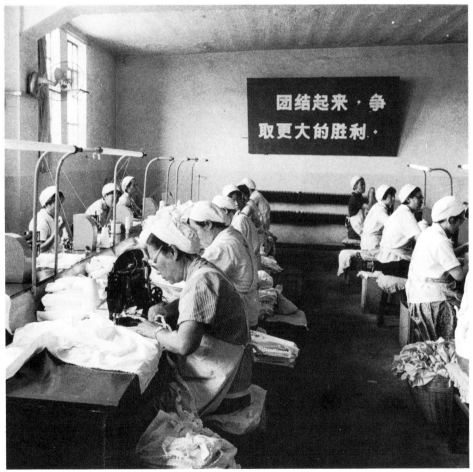

A housewives' factory in Tientsin, China, where machine-embroidered aprons, pillowslips and tablecloths are produced.

One of the most important industries in the EEC is textiles. This industry employs 10% of the workforce and accounts for 7% of the turnover of manufacturing industry. In addition, it plays a key role in providing jobs for women. About 30% of the women employed in manufacturing are textile workers.

If you live in the EEC, you soon realize that the industry is having problems. Every shirt or dress seems to have a foreign label on it such as 'Made in Hong Kong' or 'Made in Taiwan'. The clothing stores are bursting with the latest fashions imported from the Far East and Third World countries.

The EEC is still the largest importer and exporter of textiles in the world, but the Community is facing tough competition from foreign firms. Since 1973, EEC textile and clothing production has fallen by 7%; over 4,000 factories have closed down and one million jobs have been lost because of competition from other countries.

European producers cannot compete with foreign suppliers because labour costs are so much higher in Europe. A study of international labour costs was made in 1977. It showed that labour costs in some countries were 30 times greater than in others. Today, this ratio of 30:1 is about the same. A look at the chart shows that labour costs in Belgium are $8 an hour, while in Pakistan they are only ¢28.

In the past, Third World manufacturers were helped by a special international agreement—the MFA or Multifibre Arrangement—which was first introduced in 1973. The aim was to control trade in textiles among member countries, and to protect the interests of industrialized and developing nations.

Under the agreement, exporters from developing countries were allowed to increase their sales to Europe (and other markets) by 6% each year. However, if necessary, the industrialized nations of Europe could make arrangements with individual exporting countries to limit imports of certain products.

At first some countries were slow to make agreements, so firms from developing countries increased their share of EEC markets. In 1977 there was a second MFA. After that, the EEC tried harder to protect its textile industries by using other methods, including quotas, to reduce imports.

Some EEC countries, for example Germany, Holland and Denmark, do not want controls on textile imports. Others, like France, Italy and Britain, believe they need controls to protect their textile industries. All agree, however, that textile exports are vital for developing countries. The industry creates employment, and earns the foreign currency needed to pay for imported machinery and materials. Textile manufacturing offers good opportunities for people wishing to set up small businesses. As wage rates are low, not a lot of capital is needed to start up, and, as the business grows, more labour is employed.

A Comprehension

1. Why is the textile industry important in:

   a) the EEC?

   b) developing and Third World countries?

2. Which facts show that the EEC textile industries have suffered from foreign competition?

3. What does the chart tell us about:

   a) Belgium and France?

   b) Norway and Tunisia?

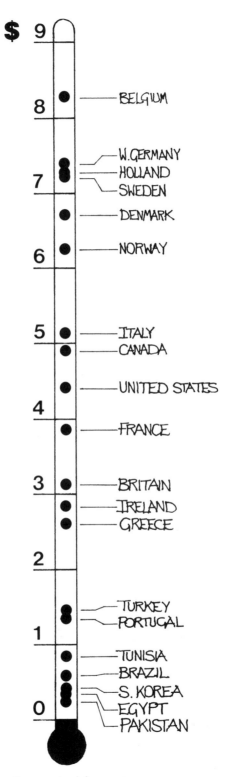

Comparative labour costs.

4. What is the MFA? How did it help the developing nations?

5. When did the EEC change its attitude towards the developing countries? Why did it do this?

6. What reasons can you give for *not* protecting the EEC's textile industries?

B Vocabulary

1. In this text, the owner of a textile business talks about his firm's activities. Read it, then do the exercises.

'We produce fashion fabrics for European clothing manufacturers and ready-to-wear garments for chain stores and mail-order companies. The manufacturers place bulk orders with us and we make the fabrics according to their specifications. Our fabrics are of first-class quality. This is because
5 we have modern dyeing techniques, a skilled labour force and good quality control.

Our ready-to-wear garments are mainly basic clothes in traditional styles. We rely on big orders and long production runs to keep prices down. At peak periods—for example, when the January sales are on—we subcontract
10 some of our work.

Recently the ready-to-wear market has become very competitive. Foreign suppliers have been undercutting us, and offering big discounts and better terms of payment. We may have to upgrade our products so that they appeal to the fashion-conscious customers in the expensive stores. In that
15 case, we shall have shorter production runs and will need to create more stylish merchandise which costs more. We shall have to look for new markets and different channels of distribution.'

a) What do these words or phrases mean?

bulk orders (l. 3)
according to their specifications (l. 3)
peak periods (l. 9)
subcontract (l. 9)
stylish merchandise (l. 16)
different channels of distribution (l. 17)

b) Find the words or phrases in the text which are close in meaning to the following:
(i)   clothes
(ii) methods of colouring material
(iii) checks and inspections of a product during its manufacture
(iv) money taken off the full price of goods
(v)   improve the quality of
(vi) people who wear up-to-date clothes

2. Look at the example. Then, complete the chart by writing correct forms of the other words.

Verb	Adjective	Nouns	
sell	selling	seller	sale
produce	. . . . . .	. . . . . .	. . . . . .
manufacture	. . . . . .	. . . . . .	. . . . . .
export	. . . . . .	. . . . . .	. . . . . .
compete	. . . . . .	. . . . . .	. . . . . .
supply	. . . . . .	. . . . . .	. . . . . .
distribute	. . . . . .	. . . . . .	. . . . . .
advertise	. . . . . .	. . . . . .	. . . . . .
market	. . . . . .	. . . . . .	. . . . . .
design	. . . . . .	. . . . . .	. . . . . .
create	. . . . . .	. . . . . .	. . . . . .

C Language Practice

Ratios

Labour costs in some countries were *thirty times more than* in others.

Here are two other ways of expressing ratios:

The clothing industry employs *ten times as many people as* the farming industry.

They import *five times as much clothing as* they did ten years ago.

Read the following and complete the exercises.

The table below gives figures for two ladies' clothing manufacturers—Carlton Dresses and Anna Wear.

	Carlton Dresses	Anna Wear
Workforce	100	800
Machinists' pay	$1 per hour	$6 per hour
Cutters' pay	$1.50 per hour	$9 per hour
Production per day		
Dresses	500	3000
Blouses	200	800
Skirts	300	600
Average ex-works prices		
Dresses	$4	$24
Blouses	$2	$10
Skirts	$6	$18
Exports per annum		
Dresses	100,000	500,000
Blouses	50,000	150,000
Skirts	25,000	100,000

Answer the questions about Carlton Dresses and Anna Wear as in the examples.

Examples:

How many people does Anna Wear employ?
They employ eight times as many people as Carlton Dresses.

How much more does a machinist at Anna Wear earn?
She earns six times as much as a machinist at Carlton Dresses.
Or
She earns six times more than a machinist at Carlton Dresses.

Questions:

How much does a cutter at Anna Wear earn?
How many dresses does Anna Wear make a day?
How much does an Anna Wear dress cost?
How many dresses does Anna Wear export a year?

Work in pairs

Using the table, ask and answer questions about the blouses and skirts.

D Oral Work

Preparation   Chairing a meeting

Christine White is an Australian. Since 1980, she has been managing director of a Portuguese textile firm, Nova Fabrics. She is chairing a meeting of her management team. Read or listen to the dialogue.

Christine: Right, can we get started please, everybody? Today we're going to talk about our plans for the future. Perhaps I should say our future strategy. Most of you know that recently we've had bad news from two of our biggest customers. Bontemps, in France, have cancelled a large order for our shirts and Blewitt stores are reducing their order for our spring dresses by 50%. This is obviously very serious for us. Does it mean that we must think again about our production and marketing objectives? Should we change our approach in some way? Ignacio, what do you think?

Ignacio: Well, could I start by saying what our problem is?

Christine: Go ahead.

Ignacio: In my view, we can't compete with these foreign manufacturers. Compete with their prices, that is. So we're losing business to them.

Christine: Who exactly do you have in mind? Hong Kong companies? Thailand? Indonesia?

Ignacio: Oh, there are so many of these low-cost firms. Even the Brazilians and Chinese have entered the market. And the Koreans, well, they seem to be everywhere these days.

Christine: That's why we're losing orders, in your view?

Ignacio: Absolutely. I tell you this, if we go into Blewitt's stores next April, half the dresses will have 'Made in Korea' on them.

Christine: Mmm, I wonder what other people think. Rosa, what's your view? Do you agree with Ignacio?

Rosa: Not completely. It's true that we're facing tough competition, but there's something we shouldn't forget. Our products are better than theirs. Our finishing and stitching are superior, and our tailoring is more professional.

Christine: What you're saying is that we offer a quality product even if our prices are a little higher. . . . Hmm, interesting. . . . Paul, would you care to comment?

Practise these expressions

To start the meeting:

Examples:

Right, can we get started please, everybody?
Right, let's get down to business, shall we?

To introduce the subject for discussion:

Examples:

Today, we're going to talk about our sales performance.
What I want to discuss today is quality control.

To remind people of the facts:

Examples:

As you know, our sales have been disappointing recently.
Most of you know that our firm is in financial difficulties.

To ask for opinions:

Examples:

Pedro, what do you think?
Maria, would you like to comment?

Work in small groups. You are all members of the same clothing firm and must attend meetings on these subjects:

a) customers' complaints of late deliveries;

b) poor quality of finished goods;

c) high labour turnover;

d) staff training.

Take turns being chairman and practise using the listed expressions.

1. Let's start now, shall we, everyone?
   May I have your attention please?

2. Today we're going to talk about . . .
   What I want to discuss today is . . .

3. As you probably know . . .
   Let me remind you all that . . .

4. . . . What do you think?
   . . . What's your opinion?
   . . . How do you feel about this?

Problem

Nova Fabrics is a Portuguese textile and clothing firm. It employs 200 workers and has a turnover of £6 million. Its management team are Europeans, except for its chief executive, Christine White, who is Australian.

The company exports almost all its production. Just under 60% of its sales revenue comes from fabrics. Nova specializes in cotton printed shirtings.[1] It is also well known for its fashion fabrics. It produces a wide range of these for European manufacturers.

The rest of its revenue comes from ready-to-wear clothing. These are basic garments—dresses, blouses, shirts, trousers, etc.—which offer good quality and traditional styles at low prices. They are made to specification for European chain stores, and sold under the stores' labels. Large production runs are possible because orders are large.

Over half of Nova's workforce are women. Employees earn less than most other textile workers in Europe. However, wage rates are rising because of action by trade unions.

Nova faces serious problems. In the last two years its fabric sales have remained steady, but profits have fallen sharply. This is because Pakistani and Indian suppliers have been forcing prices down. In the ready-to-wear market, the situation is worse. Competition is cut-throat. Exporters from 24 low-cost countries are fighting for a share of the European market. Nova is suffering from this competition. The stores are now bargaining hard over prices, and Nova has already lost two large orders.

Christine White and her management team are studying the problem carefully. Several possible solutions have been proposed. The team will discuss these at their next meeting.

What do you think?

Nova's managing director leads the discussion. The purpose of the meeting is: (i) to discuss the possible solutions (*see below*); (ii) to decide on a new production/sales strategy for the company.

Instructions:

One of you chairs the meeting. The rest of you divide into *four small groups*.

[1]This is the material used for making shirts.

Each group is given *one* of the solutions. You must propose that particular solution at the meeting and argue in favour of it. You should criticize the proposals of the other groups.

The four proposals:

1. *Stop making ready-to-wear clothing; specialize in fabrics*

   Nova will never be able to compete successfully with foreign firms in the ready-to-wear market. Therefore, it should get out of that market as soon as possible. The company should manufacture *only* fabrics. To increase sales and profits, it should expand its fabric output, make a wider range of products and look for new markets (the United States, perhaps, or Japan). At the same time, it should invest in modern technology and machinery.

2. *Move upmarket by producing more expensive, fashionable clothes*

   The firm should make a different type of product. It should manufacture more expensive, fashionable garments, selling them to high-class department stores and fashion houses. It could display the clothing at exhibitions and trade fairs. To create exciting styles, Nova should hire several new designers—people who are big names in the field of high fashion.

3. *Make no major changes; try to create a brand image for its clothes*

   Nova should continue to produce the same type of clothes but spend much more money on advertising its merchandise. The advertising should underline the excellent quality of its products—much better than that of its competitors. The company should also persuade stores to sell its products under a Nova label. This would help to establish a brand image for its clothing. Finally, Nova should plan promotions with other Portuguese textile firms and share market information.

4. *Join (merge) with another company*

   Nova should merge with another clothing manufacturer. It should look for a smaller, profitable company which has creative designers and a good marketing department. These would help to improve Nova's clothing styles and sales techniques. A merger would make it stronger financially. It could afford, then, to invest in up-to-date technology. For example, it could buy special cutting machines, controlled by computers. These greatly reduce material costs.

Additional Discussion Topics

1. In some countries, wage rates are very high; in others, they are low. How can textile firms with high wage costs compete successfully against those with low costs?

2. Why do so many textile workers in developed and developing countries earn low wages and have poor working conditions?

KAUFHAUS

1 Parade Platz   5 June, 19--
Frankfurt 8
Tel. 885280

Dear Sirs,

While attending the International Clothing and Textile
Fair in Paris last month, I saw some wool suits
manufactured by your firm. I believe they were part
of your Executive range. I am thinking of placing an
order for some of the suits and therefore would be
grateful if you would send me your catalogue, a price
list and details of your terms of payment.

In particular I wish to know the following:

> 1. Do you offer discounts (a) if customers settle
>   accounts promptly (b) if they order in bulk?
>
> 2. How do you send goods (by rail, sea, air,
>   or road transport)?
>
> 3. How soon could you deliver to Frankfurt?
>
> 4. Do you offer credit terms to new customers?
>
> 5. Do you make other garments - for men or
>   women - which would sell well in a high-class
>   store?

I look forward to receiving an early reply from you.

Yours faithfully,

Hans Muller

Hans Muller,

Chief Buyer

E Writing Exercise

You are the sales manager of a clothing company based in Lancashire, England. You have just received this letter of enquiry (see opposite). Mr Muller is chief buyer of a store in Frankfurt, West Germany.

Instructions:

Write a suitable reply to Mr Muller's letter.

F Listening Comprehension

Listen to the dialogue. Then, listen again, noting down the main facts. Finally, complete the sentences with information from the tape.

1. When Barbara was in Oxford Street, she noticed that . . . . . .
2. Between January and September, almost one million dresses . . . .
3. The shipments of dresses stopped because . . . .
4. Barbara believed that foreign firms weren't allowed . . . .
5. The purpose of the MFA is to . . . .
6. Members of the MFA include: . . . .
7. The EEC can limit the import of a particular product by . . . .
8. At present, South Korea is allowed to export to Britain about . . . .
9. British manufacturers will probably be happy because . . . .
10. Tony thinks that clothing firms will still have competition from South Korea because . . . . He admires the Koreans. In his opinion, they are . . . .

13 MULTINATIONALS AND THE THIRD WORLD

Big foreign companies—like Coca-Cola and Ford—have set up subsidiaries in many developing countries. How can the subsidiaries benefit these countries? Is this kind of investment always useful? (Explain your answer.)

Multinationals are large international companies which produce goods in several countries. Some well-known ones are Ford, Shell, Coca-Cola, Sony, Akzo and Unilever. Their turnover is huge, being greater in some cases than the national income of countries such as Switzerland or the Netherlands. Because they are so
5 big they attract a lot of attention. Usually their business methods are carefully watched by foreign governments.

People are particularly interested in their activities in poor and developing countries. They ask the question: How have multinationals improved the economies of these countries? In reply, a manager working in a multinational will
10 say something like this:

'Well, for a start, we provide the capital which poor countries need for their economic growth. The point I'm trying to make is that our capital, together with local savings, finances their industries. Another thing, we share our technology with local business—we introduce our scientific and technical methods to them.
15 And they increase the productivity of their workers.

Don't forget also that we produce a wide variety of goods. And let's face it, we employ thousands of people all over the world. No one can accuse us of not paying good wages. So, I think you'll agree, we're responsible for raising living standards.'

Critics of multinationals do not accept such arguments. They say that the big corporations are not major suppliers of capital. In Latin America, for example, multinationals have mostly used capital provided by local banks and investors, and have not brought in capital from the United States and Europe. Because of this, there is a shortage of money to finance local businesses. Foreign firms have taken the lion's share of the available capital.

The critics agree that multinationals introduce new technology. However, it is often unsuitable for developing countries. The imported technology is too expensive and complicated. It has been developed for industrial societies, not for poor countries. In agriculture, for instance, most countries do not need tractors, which are expensive to buy and operate. They need better hoes and ox-ploughs.

Another disadvantage of the new technology is that it will probably reduce jobs. Generally it is labour saving. This is because it comes from the United States and Europe where wage costs are high. Poor countries can do without such technology—they have large numbers of workers looking for employment.

Two examples prove this point. The building industry used to provide many jobs in the Third World. Now it employs fewer new workers because cranes, bulldozers and other labour-saving machinery are replacing men. And in Latin America bigger farms are using expensive imported machinery to increase production—but employing fewer and fewer workers.

A Comprehension

1. Which fact in the first paragraph emphasizes the *size* of multinationals?

2. According to the multinationals, they bring certain benefits to poor and developing countries. What, briefly, are those benefits?

3. What criticism of Latin American banks is made in lines 20–25?

4. Agricultural workers in the Third World often find their condition is made worse by the actions of multinationals. Explain this statement.

5. What are the following tools or machines used for?
   a) a hoe
   b) an ox-plough
   c) a tractor
   d) a crane
   e) a bulldozer

B Vocabulary

1. Here is part of an interview with the vice-president of a multinational corporation. Read it, then do the exercises.

Interviewer: Why did your company go multinational?

Vice-president: Mainly, I suppose, because we could no longer expand in the domestic market. It became saturated. So we moved overseas.

Interviewer: Any other reason?

Vice-president: Yes, in a number of foreign markets there were high tariffs on our goods, and in others the government was operating a quota system. In certain areas, our distributors were having trouble getting import licences. The answer was to set up a subsidiary, or have an affiliate, in those countries.

Interviewer: Let's talk about your subsidiaries. Are they independent? Can they take any decision they want?

Vice-president: Certainly not. Important decisions are taken by the parent company—that's to say, by the board of directors at our headquarters in Chicago. By important decisions, I mean things like appointing senior personnel, approving major investment plans, and so on. . . . Of course, to make the right decisions, we need good feedback from our overseas companies . . . . But, having said that, yes, our subsidiaries are fairly independent—they do their own pricing of products, hire local staff, that sort of thing. In those respects, our organization is decentralized.

Interviewer: A final question. What's your biggest headache?

Vice-president: To maintain good relations with governments so that our companies won't be nationalized.

Interviewer: Does that happen often?

Vice-president: No, but it's always possible, especially when local firms no longer need our technology or expertise. To avoid nationalization, we usually try to arrange a joint venture with a local enterprise.

a) Find words or phrases in the text which mean:
   (i)   no possibility of increasing sales
   (ii)   taxes on imported goods
   (iii)   persons who supply goods in a particular area, often to retailers
   (iv)   high-level staff
   (v)   information passed back to someone
   (vi)   not controlled by headquarters
   (vii)   taken over by the government
   (viii) expert knowledge and skill

b) What do these words or phrases mean?
   a quota system
   import licences
   affiliate
   parent company
   a joint venture with a local enterprise

2. Complete this passage by using the words in italics.

   attitude equity incentives investors levels prosperity dominate employ train set up bring out

   Countries in the Third World have different approaches to foreign investment. Some welcome foreign firms, encouraging them to . . . . subsidiaries by offering them tax . . . . . . or cheap loans. These countries believe that the foreign firms will provide jobs, pay good wages, ... local workers, bring new technology, and contribute to their . . . . . .
      Other countries have a different . . . . . . to foreign investment. They know that they need the multinationals, but they do not want these firms to . . . . . . important sectors of their economies. Therefore, they . . . . laws which force foreign companies to sell shares to local . . . . They insist that local businessmen own a certain percentage of the foreign firm's . . . . Some governments also make the foreign firm . . . . . . a certain percentage of local workers at all . . . . . . in the company.

C Language Practice

Reported speech
Vice-President: 'Important decisions *are taken* by the parent company.'
The Vice-President *said* important decisions *were taken* by the parent company.
   Notice that when the reporting verb is in the past, the other verbs must also be in the past.

Look at the following changes:

Vice-President: 'Our distributors *were having* trouble getting licences.'
He *said* their distributors *had been having* trouble getting licences.

Interviewer: 'Can subsidiaries take any decision they *want*?'
He *asked if* subsidiaries *could* take any decision they *wanted*.

Exercise 1

Put these questions, which the interviewer, Mr Miller, asked Mr Gill, a manager for a multinational, into reported speech.
Use the reporting forms in brackets as in the example.

Example:

How much of your subsidiary's profits do you re-invest? (*want to know*)
Mr Miller wanted to know how much of their subsidiary's profits they re-invested.

1. Mr Gill, do you believe multinationals have helped developing countries? (*want to know if*)
2. Do multinationals take the lion's share of the available capital? (*ask*)
3. Why did some countries nationalize subsidiaries in the 1970s? (*wonder*)
4. Can it be said that multinationals are major suppliers of capital? (*want to know if*)
5. What is a multinational able to offer a developing country? (*ask*)
6. When were your company's first subsidiaries set up? (*want to know*)
7. Will multinationals have to offer developing countries better terms? (*want to know whether*)
8. Who has benefited from your company's subsidiaries? (*ask*)

Exercise 2

Put these statements made by Mr Gill, the manager working for a multinational, into reported speech. Use the reporting verbs in brackets.

'Our new subsidiary will provide work for hundreds of people.' (*claim*)

'I do not know of any worker who is not happy at our plant.' (*say*)

'People often have the wrong idea about multinationals.' (*complain*)

'We will train local staff for management positions.' (*promise*)

'The government will be pleased with our results.' (*feel sure*)

'We can expect good relations with the government to continue.' (*think*)

'Our company is going to set up another subsidiary there.' (*explain*)

'We made a record profit in September.' (*announce*)

Exercise 3

Put Mr Gill's comments below into reported speech. Use each verb in the list only once.

explained denied promised asked claimed complained

a) 'We do not pay low wages.'

b) 'Because local business shares our technology, it increases productivity.'

c) 'We will help local business in every way we can.'

d) 'Unpleasant things are often said about us in the press.'

e) 'Do people really believe we are preventing local firms from growing?'

f) 'Our subsidiaries are a real benefit to developing countries.'

D Oral Work

Preparation Expressing future plans and intentions/making criticisms

Max works for an international pharmaceutical company. He is regional manager for Africa. For the past 10 years he has been based in an important African country—we shall call it Bakumba. Here, he is talking to his wife, Paula, who is angry and upset.

Paula: Listen to me, Max. I'm not going to take it any more. I'm fed up with Bakumba and our whole life here. The boring parties we go to, you always complaining about your job. I warn you, I'm going to walk out soon.

Max: Oh, come on, darling, don't you think you're being a bit unreasonable? If you'll only be patient, I'm sure I can work something out.

Paula: Patient? You must be joking. Look, we've been here more than 10 years. You told me you were going to be promoted. You said they intended to make you a director, in New York or Geneva. And here we are . . . still stuck in Bakumba. You lied to me, Max.

Max: That's not fair, Paula, and you know it. How was I to know they'd promote younger people over my head?

Paula: Don't you understand, Max, I want to live a little. I'm only 30, for God's sake. It's different for you, you're . . .

Max: OK, OK, I'm almost 50. You needn't go on about it.

Paula: I didn't mean it like that, honestly.

Max: I know you didn't, darling . . . I don't blame you, really. It's a lousy life for you here, but believe me . . .

Paula: Yes?

Max: I'm going to do something about it.

Paula: Really, Max?

Max: I promise you. I intend to make them send us back to Europe or the States.

Paula: But how? They do just what they like, don't they? They don't listen to anyone.

Max: They will, Paula, you'll see. I'm planning to make things very difficult for them in the future.

Practise these expressions:

To talk about future plans/intentions:

Examples:

I'm going to change my job soon.
I intend to talk to my boss about this matter.
I'm planning to ask for an increase in salary.

To criticize somebody (or criticize their attitudes):

Examples:

Don't you think you're being rather unwise/silly/selfish?
Aren't you being rather unrealistic?

Five people are about to be made redundant by their firm. Below, they are talking about their future plans with friends. Complete the dialogues with suitable comments.

1. A: As soon as I leave this job, I'm going to . . . .
   B: Are you sure that's the best thing to do?

2. A: First, I intend to have a holiday abroad—without the family, if possible.
   B: Don't you think you're being . . . . . . ?

3. A: If I have difficulty finding another job, I'm planning to . . . .
   B: Don't you think you're being . . . .?

4. A: I may be only 40, but I intend to stop working for good.
   B: Oh come on now, aren't you being . . . . . . ?

5. A: After I've had a short rest, I propose to . . . .
   B: That's very sensible, I must say.

Problem

Max works for an international pharmaceutical company. He is regional manager for Africa and is based in Bakumba. He has been in his present position for the past 10 years. His wife, Paula, is a lot younger than him. She hates living in Bakumba, and will probably leave her husband if they cannot return to New York or Geneva.

Important decisions in the company are taken by the board of directors in New York. The board consists of a president and five other members. The staff call them the 'Big Six'. When the president appointed Max, he said: 'If you do well in Africa, there will be a place for you on one of our boards—in Tokyo perhaps, or Mexico City.'

Max is now over 50 years old. In recent years, younger men have been promoted to those boards. In his heart, Max knows that he has missed the boat.

The African markets are extremely profitable for the company. The Bakumban subsidiary makes more money than all the other subsidiaries. The reasons for this are as follows:

1. The company sells many common drugs at very high prices. It makes 800–1,000% profit on most of them. It can do this because the drugs are protected by patents.

2. It sells drugs which are completely useless. However, because it advertises them heavily, the Bakumbans buy them.

3. It markets other drugs which cannot be sold in Europe or the United States because they are dangerous to people's health.

4. It does not supply any drug which is expensive to manufacture, even though that drug may save the lives of people in Bakumba.

Max knows all these secrets about the company. Now, he intends to set up a meeting with the board of directors in New York. They will be surprised when they hear what he has to say to them.

What do you think?

Max has come to New York to meet the board of directors. He is accompanied by a friend who is a journalist for a Bakumban newspaper.

At the meeting, Max will put pressure on the directors to send him back to Europe or the United States. His friend will back him up. After listening to Max, the directors must decide how to deal with the situation. Read the notes for your roles before starting the meeting.

Roles:

Directors

The president leads the discussion. You know that Max wishes to return to Europe or the United States. He will put pressure on you to send him back. However, you want Max to stay in Bakumba until he retires. He is an excellent regional manager, but he is not suited to be a director. Be tough with him—but be careful. Don't make any decision that will be bad for the company. Remember, Bakumba is your biggest market.

Max

You want the directors to send you back to Europe or the United States. If they refuse, you will put pressure on them. You will warn them that you will tell the Bakumbans about your company's dishonest marketing policies. Also, your friend will write newspaper articles about the company's business methods. Try to persuade the directors to do these things:

1. Send you back to Geneva or New York immediately.
2. Pay you £50,000 for all your hard work in Bakumba during the past 10 years (the directors have made this sort of payment to other executives in the past).
3. Appoint you to the board of directors in Geneva or New York.

Friend

You should back Max up in the discussion.

Additional Discussion Topics

1. Which multinational company do you most admire or dislike? Give reasons for your answer.

2. What international organizations exist to help poor and developing countries? Do these organizations do a good job?

E Writing Exercise

This letter is based on a conversation between Mr Luck and his chief packer, Mr Okele. Using information from it, write out the dialogue that took place between the two men.

---

9 July, 19--

Dear Mr Ngomo,

Order No. Y 368   Item: 600 medicine bottles

I am sorry to hear that fifty bottles in this consignment were broken. I have now looked into the matter.

I asked our chief packer, Mr Okele, if the goods had been carefully packed and checked before leaving the factory. He seemed rather annoyed by my question, but then assured me that the clerk had done his job properly. Each bottle was wrapped in cardboard, and straw had been placed in the case to stop the bottles moving during shipment. I suggested to Mr Okele that the railway workers could have caused the damage. He didn't agree, pointing out that the case was clearly marked 'DELICATE. HANDLE WITH CARE'. Mr Okele said that one of your staff may have broken the bottles when unpacking them. He asked if you could make enquiries at your end.

My chief packer insisted that we were not to blame for the damaged goods. I agreed with him and promised to tell you what he had said.

I hope this information is useful to you.

Yours sincerely,

G. Luck

G. Luck

Manager

F Listening Comprehension

This memorandum is written by the personnel director to the general manager. Complete it by writing suitable words in the spaces and by using information from the tape.

To: General Manager
From: Personnel Director   Date: 25 September 19....

Subject: Overseas posting of Isobel Harper

1. I talked to Mrs Harper about her posting to Brazil. She . . . . . . that she could not . . . . . . the posting because her daughter, Gillian, had a . . . . Her doctor had sent her to a . . . . . and she was still under his care. For this reason, Mrs Harper does not want to risk . . . . . . Gillian to Brazil.

2. I . . . . . Mrs Harper that she had the opportunity to become a director in the future. I also mentioned our personnel policy and . . . . . . to her that senior . . . . . had to spend two years at our Brazilian . . . . She then pointed out that she had another problem. Her husband had been . . . . . . recently, and therefore would not want to go to Brazil either.

3. I . . . . . Mrs Harper to think about her future carefully and . . . . . that there were good psychiatrists in Brazil who could look after her daughter. I reminded her that her husband was a . . . . He would easily get a job in Brazil.

4. Mrs Harper tried to persuade me to change our . . . . She argued that she had good reasons . . . . the overseas posting. I told her firmly that we could not treat her . . . . . . from other people. That would be unfair and might . . . . . . other executives to refuse postings. Finally, I . . . . . . her to go away and consider the matter carefully.

5. Mrs Harper . . . . . . me that she . . . . . . probably not change her mind.

14 THE MONDRAGON COOPERATIVES

Cooperatives are firms which are owned and controlled by the people who work in them. Members share in the capital of the cooperative and choose their own managers. Is this the best kind of business organization? Should all firms be organized this way?

Twenty-five years ago, five workers started a small enterprise in a valley in the Basque region of Spain. It was a workers' cooperative—that is, a business owned and controlled by the people working in it. Today it has become one of the most famous and successful cooperatives in Europe. People from all over the world
5 come to visit it, especially government and trade union officials. They think cooperatives could help to solve the problem of unemployment in their countries.

There are now not one but 75 separate cooperatives grouped round the little town of Mondragon, near Bilbao. They make a wide range of goods—everything from refrigerators and bicycles to agricultural machinery.

10 Mondragon is a success story. Over the past 25 years, they have had only one strike. Their sales record has been good, and so has their productivity. Net profits have been double those of ordinary firms. Recently, when unemployment in some parts of Spain was high, they did not lay off a single worker.

The man who started Mondragon in 1956 was a Basque priest, Father José-
15 Maria Arizmendi. He opened a technical school in the village, with money provided by local businessmen. Father José-Maria wanted to help the poor and unemployed in the area, but he believed they should improve their lives by their own efforts.

Later on he persuaded 100 villagers to invest money in a business run by a few
20 workers. When the business was on its feet, he recommended that it should be organized as a cooperative.

The first, and now the largest cooperative, ULGOR, has 3,400 employees. Its six factories produce washing machines and refrigerators. It is one of Spain's biggest manufacturers and exports 25% of its production. Over the years, four or
25 five new cooperatives have opened up every year.

Mondragon's savings bank, the Caja Laboral, has played a key role in that growth. Its 64 branches attract savings from the Basque people, which are invested in the cooperatives. The bank considers suggestions for new projects and, if it approves, helps finance and plan them. It also keeps an eagle eye on the
30 cooperatives' managers, carefully monitoring their performance.

Headquarters of the Caja Laboral Popular, Mondragon, Spain.

A new cooperative is financed in this way. Each member who joins pays £2,000. Then the government contributes about 20% of its capital from a special fund. Finally about 60% comes from the bank. Each worker is paid a monthly salary. The highest-paid person never gets more than three times the lowest-paid worker.

35 Workers share in the cooperative's management, and in its capital. They choose the board of directors, which appoints a general manager. The board consists of both skilled and unskilled workers. No one is paid extra to be a director.

A Comprehension

1. Which facts show that the cooperatives of Mondragon have grown at a fast rate?

2. How successful are the cooperatives compared with other Spanish companies? Explain your answer.

3. Father José-Maria advised the workers to organize their business as a cooperative. Why do you think he made this suggestion?

4. What do these words or phrases mean?
   net profits (l. 11)
   the business was on its feet (l. 20)
   a key role (l. 26)
   keeps an eagle eye on (l. 29)
   carefully monitoring their performance (l. 30)

5. Analyse the reasons for Mondragon's success.

B Vocabulary

1. Fill in the correct *form* of the given words in these sentences:

   Example: The Bank makes many *RECOMMENDATIONS* to the managers
   of cooperatives. (*recommend*)

   a) There will be further . . . . . . at Mondragon in future years. (*expand*)

   b) Cooperatives may provide a . . . . . . to the problem of unemployment.
   (*solve*)

   c) The bank plays an important role in the . . . . . . of new cooperatives. (*plan*)

   d) So far, there has not been a single . . . . . . of a cooperative enterprise. (*fail*)

   e) In most companies, ... is in the hands of shareholders, who do not work
   in the business. (*own*)

   f) The . . . . . . of most cooperatives has been excellent. (*perform*)

   g) One of Father José-Maria's . . . . . . was that 'knowledge is power'. (*believe*)

   h) Final . . . . . . for a project is given by the bank's managerial division.
   (*approve*)

   i) Constant . . . . . . of the cooperatives' performance is carried out by the
   bank. (*monitor*)

   j) Most people are surprised by the rapid . . . . . . of cooperatives. (*grow*)

2. Below, an expert on banking is talking about the activities of Mondragon's
   bank, the Caja Laboral. Work in pairs. Discuss what each of the words or
   phrases in italics means. Then, compare your answers with those of other
   pairs in your group.

   'The bank is the *nerve centre* of the Mondragon cooperatives. It not only
   finances them, but is also responsible for planning and *launching* them. Its
   managerial division considers ideas for new projects and carries out
   feasibility studies. If necessary, it will arrange for market research surveys. If
   it is satisfied with its *findings*, it will give the final *go-ahead*. After that, the
   bank looks for a suitable *site* for the project. It contacts architects to design
   the factory, looks for personnel to run it, and even buys machinery to install
   in it.

   Although the workers have the power to *hire and fire* managers, it is the
   bank which often has the *final say* in such matters. When the cooperative is
   in operation, the bank receives a constant *flow of data* from its management.
   If there are problems, it puts forward proposals for solving them.'

C Language Practice

Third conditional
Because Father José-Maria Arizmendi started a cooperative, *he helped to reduce*
unemployment in the region.
   This idea can be expressed like this:
If Father José-Maria Arizmendi had not started a cooperative, *he would not have
helped to reduce* unemployment in the region.

Read the following and complete Exercise 1.

There are many cooperatives in India. Two Indian cooperatives went to the bank with projects for which they wanted financial backing. The bank approved one project but rejected the other.

Here are the notes the head of the bank's investment section made on the project the bank approved.

Project: Small bicycle factory.
High technology not required for this project.
Demand for bicycles is high in India.
Materials do not have to be imported.
The project provides work for other local tradesmen.
The project does not require many skilled workers.
It does not take long to set up such a project.
We expect a return on our investment within two years.
There is no other bicycle factory in the region.

Five years after the project started a bank spokesman said:

'We would not have approved the project if high technology had been required.'

'We would have rejected the project if demand for bicycles had been low in India.'

Exercise 1
Make similar comments.

Read the following and complete Exercise 2.

The second project was a deep-sea diving equipment factory. The bank refused to finance this project.

Here are some of the comments the head of the bank's investment section made to a colleague, after the bank had turned down the project.

'The bank did not approve the project, because demand for deep-sea diving equipment is not high in India.'

'The bank turned down their request, as the project required a lot of skilled labour.'

'We did not support the project, because it did not provide work for other local tradesmen.'

'India does not produce many of the materials needed, so we turned down the project.'

'It costs a lot to set up such a project, so we did not want to help.'

'We refused their request, since the bank could not recover their investment in under five years.'

'Many other countries produce cheap diving equipment, so we were not interested in the idea.'

'We did not consider the idea a safe investment, as the project depended on demand from foreign distributors.'

Exercise 2

Rewrite his comments in the third conditional as in the example.

Example:

The bank would have approved the project if demand for deep-sea diving equipment had been high in India.

D Oral Work

Preparation   Chairing a meeting

This meeting is between the managers and shopfloor workers in an industrial cooperative. The firm makes a special type of iron used in the steel industry. Members are talking about the problem of dust in the cast house. This is the part of the factory where iron is made into different shapes and sizes. Read or listen to the dialogue.

Plant manager:	Am I right in saying, Ted, you consider this dust to be a danger to our workers' health?
Medical officer:	Well, I think that it could be, yes. It's strange you know, in the last few years several people working in the cast house have suffered from chest and lung diseases. The kind you get from breathing in dust.
Plant manager:	Mmm, this is very worrying. Would anyone like to comment? Yes, Don?
Production manager:	I'd like to make a suggestion. I think we should start measuring dust levels in the area, and also consider ways of protecting people from this hazard.
Plant manager:	That's a good idea, Don. Jeff, do you want to say something?
Foreman:	I'd just like to say, I'm not surprised to hear that the dust is dangerous. I've been telling you for a long time that we need to be more careful about health and safety in this factory. Look at Charlie last week, almost killed by an electric shock.
Plant manager:	You're right, Jeff, but can we come back to the point, please? We're talking about dust hazards, not electrical ones. Now, does anyone else wish to say anything? Rosalind?
Personnel officer:	If Ted's right, and this dust has affected the health of the cast house workers, we'd better start thinking about paying them compensation, don't you think?
Plant manager:	Mmm . . . it could cost a lot of money.
Personnel officer:	Maybe, but if they've become ill because of bad working conditions, surely we must . . .
Plant manager:	I think we could consider the question of compensation at a later meeting. I agree you've made an important point, Rosalind. Any

further comments? Jack? Susan? No . . . ? Right, are we all agreed, then? We should measure dust levels in the cast house, and look into ways of protecting our workers. Later on, we'll consider compensating those whose health has been affected. Good, that's all for today, thank you, ladies and gentlemen.

Practise these expressions

To keep people talking about the subject:

Examples:

Can we get/come back to the point, please?
Can we come back to that later, please?

To bring an end to the discussion:

Examples:

Does anyone else wish to say anything?
Are there any other points?

To confirm general agreement:

Examples:

Right, are we all agreed then?
Right, we all seem to agree that we need new machinery.

To close the meeting:

Examples:

That's all for today, thank you, ladies and gentlemen.
I think we can call it a day.

Here are several comments made by a chairman during a meeting. Rearrange the comments so that you show the probable *order* in which they were made.

Are there any further comments?

Well, that seems to be about all. Thank you very much, ladies and gentlemen.

Today, we're going to discuss rates of pay.

Thank you, John. Now let's see. Susan, would you like to comment?

Let me remind you that the rates we pay are above average for our industry.

Right, we all seem to agree that our rates of pay need revising.

May I have your attention please, everyone?

John, would you like to start the ball rolling?

Very interesting, Tom, but could we get back to the point, please?

Problem

The cooperative makes a special kind of iron, which is used by the steel industry when very hard-wearing materials are needed, as in parts of aeroplane engines. Because of the process used to mould the iron, dust collects in the air of the cast house. This is breathed in by the workers and may be causing some of them to have diseases of the chest and lungs.

The cooperative was started in 1965. It has done well since then, mainly because it produces a small range of highly specialized products and materials. It has a workforce of 600 and a large annual turnover. However, nowadays it is having to keep costs down and reduce its profit margins. New firms are entering the field and competition is keen. During the past nine months the plant has been working at 30% below capacity.

The health and safety officer has carried out a careful study of the dust problem in the cast house. Special equipment has been installed, which samples the dust every hour during the working day. A team of experts from a private industrial research organization has visited the cooperative. Its report is now in the hands of the health and safety officer. It contains an estimate of the cost of creating a dust-free atmosphere on the cast house floor.

The plant manager has called another meeting. This time it will be chaired by the health and safety officer, who will present his/her plan for solving the problem. He/she will then invite other people at the meeting to give their views. Finally, those present will decide what action to take in this situation.

What do you think?

The health and safety officer chairs the meeting. Each of you plays one of the roles described below. The purpose of the meeting is to decide how to cope with the problem of dust in the cast house.

Roles:

Health and safety officer
You have studied carefully the results of the air tests and the report of the team of experts. You should give this information at the meeting.

1. The levels of dust in the cast house area are, at certain times, very high. They are much higher than those allowed by government factory inspectors.

2. It is probable that the workers' health has been harmed by the dust. However, it is difficult to prove this.

3. To create a dust-free atmosphere, the cooperative would have to spend several million pounds. It would have to:
   a) install expensive ventilation equipment to suck out the dust;
   b) change the process it is now using. It would need to automate part of the production and buy costly new equipment;
   c) set up a system of frequent air testing.

You think the cooperative should spend as much money as necessary to reduce dust levels in the cast house.

Plant manager
If the cooperative spends too much money on health and safety, it will go out of business. Then no one will have a job. Suggest that the cooperative buys face masks and protective clothing for the workers. In your opinion, expenditure on dust control should be limited.

Financial director

You do not want the cooperative to spend money on reducing dust levels. At the moment, it must reduce costs, not dust! Point out that this process for making iron has always created dust. Government inspectors know this and are very understanding about the problem.

Worker representatives

You are in favour of spending a lot of money on dust control. There should be more medical examinations for workers. The cooperative should provide protective clothing, such as face masks. However, remind members that workers often take off face masks because the cast house is so hot.

Foremen

You are in favour of reducing dust levels. You believe that it is impossible to create a dust-free atmosphere—even if you spend millions of pounds on air-cleaning equipment.

Personnel officer

You do not want the cooperative to spend huge sums of money on dust control. To have dust-free air, it will have to automate certain parts of the production process. Many workers may then lose their jobs. Remind members about the compensation payments for workers—these will cost a lot of money.

Medical officer

The cooperative has a duty to protect its workers. It must spend as much money as necessary to do this. You want it to install expensive air-cleaning equipment and to increase the size of your medical department. It must have a programme of air tests and medical supervision of workers.

Additional Discussion Topics

1. What types of health hazards are caused by companies? How can people be protected against them?
2. Have there been any cases in your country of firms causing health or safety hazards? If so, give details.

E Writing Exercise

The workers have asked the plant manager to give them more information about the dust hazard in the cast house. They also want to know what the management is doing to deal with the problem.

The plant manager has decided to make a short *statement* to the workers. It will consist of four paragraphs. Here are his rough notes for each part of the statement.

Para. 1. Admit that we're worried about dust levels. Refer to air tests/independent investigation by research organization. Dust levels *are* too high—we don't know for sure they harm people's health.

Para. 2. Immediate action to be taken:
     face masks ✔
     eye goggles ✔
     protective clothing ✔
Air-cleaning equipment? Perhaps later, when we know cost, efficiency of equipment, etc.

Para. 3. Special medical programme to be set up. Check-ups every six months for all workers.

Para. 4. Other actions: possibility of compensation for sick workers/transfer to other departments.

Now, write up the plant manager's statement, using the above notes.

F Listening Comprehension

Answer these questions.

1. What was Helge doing this morning?
2. Why did Francisco say, 'Good Heavens!'?
3. What has the Italian cooperative just finished doing?
4. Which countries is Somalia near to?
5. Where is Berbera? Why does Helge mention its name?
6. Why does Francisco say, 'It must have been a difficult project'?
7. How are the cooperative's managers chosen?
8. What did Helge say that she found specially interesting about the cooperative?
9. What does Helge say about salaries?
10. How does Francisco feel about cooperatives? What does he wish?

15 DIAMONDS LOSE THEIR SPARKLE

There is a well-known saying: 'Diamonds are a girl's best friend'. What does this mean? Do you think it is true?

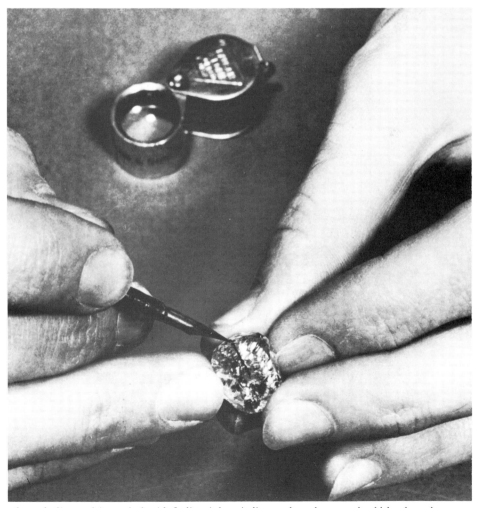

A rough diamond is marked with Indian ink to indicate where the stone should be cleaved or sawed.

De Beers is the biggest diamond producer in the world. It is a South African company, led by Mr Harry Oppenheimer, and it markets its stones through the Central Selling Organization (CSO). This body was set up in the 1930s by Oppenheimer's father. It consists of most of the major diamond producers and handles 80% of world diamond production. The CSO is dominated by the De Beers company.

Rough (uncut) diamonds are sold by the CSO at its 'sights'. These are monthly sales, attended by about 300 top dealers. At the sights the dealers can view the gems before deciding whether to buy them.

The early 1980s have been a difficult period for De Beers and the CSO. Because of bad business conditions and high interest rates, demand for diamonds has fallen. In particular, the market for high-priced investment stones has been weak. As one expert said, 'Diamonds have lost a lot of their sparkle'.

During 1981, sales by the CSO dropped by 46% to $1472 million. As a result, the organization has had to finance huge stocks of unsold rough diamonds. It guarantees to buy a minimum amount of diamonds from De Beers and the other producers each year. In this way, it can control the supply and price of the stones.

To help dealers, the CSO has been keeping—withholding—diamonds from the market. Its sights have been smaller than usual and it has tried to match the number of diamonds it offers to what dealers can sell.

Falling sales are not the CSO's only problem. In 1981, a big producer, Zaire, ended its 14-year-old contract with the organization and began selling directly to buyers. By doing this, it saved on commissions to the CSO and increased its profits by 38%.

After Zaire had left the CSO, Mr Oppenheimer was asked how he felt about it. He said, 'I can't pretend we're pleased when anyone breaks away. It's a bad example'. Perhaps he was afraid that other African countries might follow suit.

Having lost the Zaire contract, the CSO began worrying about another diamond producer—Australia. The Ashton mines in Western Australia would increase world diamond production by about 40% in 1985. But were they going to sell through the CSO? That was the big question. It now seems that De Beers will handle the marketing of about 75% of Ashton's output, once the mines are in full production.

People with inside knowledge of the industry say that De Beers have been successful because they offered a guaranteed, five-year sales contract.

Early in 1982 the fortunes of De Beers reached their lowest point. The company announced that it was cutting its annual dividend for the first time since 1944. This was because of a slump in its profits. The bad news caused De Beers' share price to drop sharply on stock exchanges throughout the world.

In spite of this, De Beers should be able to keep its leading position in the diamond business. It has large cash resources, and will be able to take advantage of better economic conditions when these come.

A Comprehension

1. Who started the CSO? What is its main purpose?
2. Why have diamonds lost their sparkle?

3. How did Mr Oppenheimer feel when Zaire left the CSO? Why did he feel like that?

4. What advantages did Zaire gain by leaving the CSO?

5. Why was De Beers particularly interested in having a contract with Ashton mines?

6. List in note form the problems of De Beers during the 1980s.

7. What do these words or phrases mean?
   investment stones (l. 12)
   I can't pretend we're pleased (l. 26)
   follow suit (l. 27)
   inside knowledge (l. 34)
   a slump in its profits (l. 38)

B Vocabulary

1. Here are some comments about diamonds by a jeweller. Fill in the gaps with words from the box. Make any changes necessary in the form of the words.

   'If you own a piece of jewellery, you may want to know what it is . . . .
   The best way to find out is to visit some jewellers. They will be willing to
   . . . . . its value for you. If you are lucky enough to own a . . . . . .
   diamond, in other words, one that has no . . . . . . at all, it will be worth a
   lot of money. Such diamonds increase in . . . . . . over the years, so they are
   a good . . . . . . for anyone who buys them. The buyer will be able to sell the
   stone at a . . . .
      Some people buy diamonds in order to sell them later at a higher price.
   They are . . . . . . in diamonds and taking a big risk. If demand for gems
   increases, they will make a profit. But if there is a slump in the market, they
   will have to sell at a . . . . Before buying a diamond, you should consult
   an expert. His advice will be . . . . He may prevent you from buying a
   stone which you think is valuable, but in fact is almost . . . . Most
   people are given diamonds by someone who loves them. Such stones are
   . . . . . . , whatever their market value may be.'

value	*invaluable*	*loss*
worth	*estimate*	*profit*
worthless	*speculate*	*defect*
priceless	*investment*	*flawless*

2. Complete the sentences with suitable words.

   a) This firm deals . . . . . . jewellery.

   b) The long-term value of diamonds depends . . . . . . better economic conditions.

   c) My company specializes . . . . . . buying jewellery from the general public.

d) In 1981, the net profits of the De Beers group fell . . . . . . 46%.

e) An increase . . . . . . diamond stocks is expected this year.

f) A world-famous diamond was recently put . . . . . . the market.

g) The mark-up on diamonds ranges . . . . . . 100% . . . . . . 200%.

h) You can get a good return . . . . . . your investment if you buy flawless stones.

i) World jewellery sales increased . . . . . . value during 1982.

j) Sometimes you have to sell things . . . . . . a loss.

k) Three years ago, diamond sales were . . . . . . a peak.

l) Retailers often receive diamonds from wholesalers . . . . . . consignment. (They do not have to pay for the stones until they have sold them.)

m) Demand for gem stones has fallen . . . . . . during the year.

n) The Ashton mine comes . . . . . . full production in 1985.

o) Top-class gems are almost always . . . . . . short supply.

C Language Practice

Tense review

The table shows details of four months' trading at the Crest Street branch of Camrose the Jewellers.

Crest St branch	Price range Low/medium/high ✓ ✓				Range of stock Modern/Reproduction/Antique ✓ ✓ ✓
	Jan	*Feb*	*Mar*	*Apr*	
Diamond rings:					
Sales for cash	50	20	60	80	
Sales on credit	70	30	120	200	
Purchases over the counter	50	20	—	10	
Repairs in shop	—	20	30	10	
Repairs sent away	10	—	40	30	

Exercise 1

You are the manager of the Crest Street branch. Use the information in the table to describe the shop you run.

Example:

I sell medium-priced diamond rings.

Exercise 2 (Work in pairs)
The area manager telephones the manager of the Crest Street branch at the end of April. Ask and answer the area manager's questions.

The area manager wants to know:
If he sold more rings for cash or on credit in January.
How many rings were bought over the counter in January.
If he did any repairs in the shop in January.
How many repairs he has done in the shop so far this year.
If he sent any repairs away in January.
How many rings have been sent away for repair since January.

What other questions can you ask and answer?

Exercise 3
'By the end of February he had sold 70 diamond rings for cash.'
Make four similar comments about February.

'When he sold the 80 rings for cash in April he had already sold 130 that year.'
Make four similar comments about April.

Exercise 4
Use the information in the table to complete the outlines below.

a) *The shop/specialize in/medium and . . . /jewellery.*

b) *In February/30 rings/sell/on . . .*

c) *He/buy/ . . . rings/the counter/April.*

d) *This year/shop/send/ . . . rings/away/repair.*

e) *By/end/January/shop/not repair/rings/ . . .*

f) *So far/year/shop/buy/ . . . rings/over . . .*

g) *Since/beginning/this year/90 repairs/send/ . . .*

h) *In March/no rings/buy/over . . .*

i) *When he/buy/the 10 rings/April/he/not buy/rings/since February.*

j) *In February/he/not send/rings away/for . . .*

D Oral Work

Preparation   Presenting a scheme enthusiastically/expressing approval

Valerie Wise is director of a New York public relations firm. She has just thought of a new scheme to get business for the company. Here, she talks about it to two other directors, Howard and Chuck. Read or listen to the dialogue.

Valerie: I've got a great idea for a new project. Do you want to hear about it, you guys?

Howard: Why not, Val? We need to find something new if we're going to stay in business much longer.

Valerie: OK then. You see, I have this friend in the diamond trade.

Chuck: Lucky you!

Valerie: Yeah, well, I'll tell you something, he's not exactly throwing diamonds in my direction at the moment—but that's another story.

Chuck: We believe you.

Valerie: Anyway, he was telling me, everybody's fed up in the trade these days.

Howard: How come?

Valerie: For one thing the big company, De Beers, is having a tough time—its profits fell by almost 50% last year. Apparently there are too many diamonds on the market, so prices are falling.

Chuck: How does that help us?

Valerie: Well, diamonds have had a lot of bad publicity lately. Several people have written books about the business. They've been very critical.

Chuck: In what way?

Valerie: Oh, they say diamonds don't hold their value. If you buy an expensive ring, and want to sell it later, you can't get much money for it.

Howard: So, 'diamonds aren't forever', then?

Valerie: You've got it. This is bad news for the merchants and big jewellery stores.

Howard: So?

Valerie: So, my idea is to approach some of the big diamond dealers. We'd offer to do a public relations job for them. They could all share the cost of the campaign.

Chuck: Yeah, I like it, Val. It's a great idea.

Valerie: I think it would work. And it would be something completely different for us. Really original. It'd offer tremendous scope for all our talents.

Howard: It could be very profitable as well.

Practise these expressions

To present a scheme enthusiastically:

Examples:

I've got a great idea for increasing our profits.
My idea is to cut our profit margins.
I've thought of a good way of getting new customers.

To show approval/disapproval for a scheme:

Examples:

That's a great idea.
That sounds really interesting.
Do you really think it'll work?

Work in small groups. First, think of a scheme that you would like to present to your group. For example, it could be a scheme for:
    making money quickly;
    changing the law in your country;
    improving people's lives;
    making your company more efficient.
    Then present your scheme to the group. Use some of the listed expressions in your discussions.
    I've thought of a good way of . . .
    My idea is . . .
    I've got a great idea for . . .
    I've just had a brainwave. Why don't we . . . ?

    That's a good idea.
    It sounds very interesting.
    Mmm, it's certainly worth trying.
    Do you really think it would work?

Problem

Valerie's scheme was a good one. A month later, she met four top New York jewellers. Two weeks after that, a second meeting took place. There were over 30 people present—diamond cutters, traders and jewellery retailers. One man dominated the discussion. This was Marcus Sugarman, an important person in the diamond world.

Mr Sugarman came straight to the point: 'You can have as much money as you like, Ms Wise. The sky's the limit. You can use any diamond in our possession. We're asking you to plan an exciting public relations campaign for our trade. We want New Yorkers to talk about diamonds again, to dream about them, and, above all, to love them. When people do that, our gems will be back in fashion again.'

Valerie replied: 'This will be a great challenge for us. I promise you, we'll come up with a spectacular campaign.'

Mr Sugarman seemed to be pleased: 'That's exactly what we need. Something really spectacular! Our business has been in a slump for two years now. It's time we did something about it.'

After the meeting, Valerie was feeling excited. Mr Sugarman had asked her company to plan a public relations campaign for the New York diamond trade. If they could think up some interesting ideas for a campaign, her firm's future would be secure.

What do you think?

The purpose of the campaign is to bring diamonds back into fashion. The campaign must create a better image for them in the minds of New Yorkers. In addition, it has to persuade the public to visit the big stores which sell diamond jewellery. The firm can use any promotional methods it wishes to achieve these aims.

You are all executives in Valerie's firm. Divide into small groups. Each group should plan a public relations campaign for diamonds for the New York area. When you have done this, meet as one large group to discuss each of the campaigns. Then, choose the best project to present to Mr Sugarman.

Additional Discussion Topics

1. Here are some things in which a person can invest money:

   (i) diamonds   (ii) modern paintings   (iii) property   (iv) shares   (v) gold

   What are the advantages and disadvantages of each type of investment? Which of the above would you choose to put money in?

2. Does De Beers play a useful role in the diamond industry?

E Writing Exercise

Next week, Valerie Wise is having another meeting with the representatives of the diamond and jewellery trade. Before doing so, she has promised to write to Mr Marcus Sugarman, giving him a brief outline of the campaign they have planned. She will explain how her firm intends to improve the image of diamonds, and to persuade people to take a greater interest in diamond jewellery.

Write the letter that Valerie sends to Mr Sugarman.

F Listening Comprehension

Here is a newspaper report of the television programme *Book a Week*. Complete the article with information from the tape. (Take notes while you listen and, if necessary, hear the tape twice.)

LIZ FARBER ON
BOOK A WEEK **PROGRAMME**

Last night, on the TV programme *Book a Week*, Elizabeth Farber, the
. . . . ., talked about a book called '. . . . .' by Mr Edward Epstein.

Ms Farber said that the book was extremely informative. It
contained, for example, many facts about . . . .

She had been particularly interested in the chapters dealing with
Russian diamonds. She told viewers that the Soviet Union used . . . . . .
to market its stones. Then, she mentioned that there was a . . . . . .
about the Russian gems.

According to the author of the book, the Russians discovered . . . . . .
in 1955, and in 1962, De Beers . . . . . ., agreeing to buy most of the
mine's output.

This Russian mine was different from other ones because . . . .
De Beers were surprised when this happened. They were also
suspicious for two reasons: first, ...; second, ...

The author of the book has a possible explanation for the mystery.
He suggests that the diamonds . . . . However, an employee of De
Beers states that . . . . Ms Faber contacted some people in the
diamond business to check the truth of the story. They seemed to think
that . . . .